COMMENTARY ON THE UNIDROIT CONVENTION ON STOLEN AND ILLEGALLY EXPORTED CULTURAL OBJECTS 1995

Lyndel V. Prott

Opinions expressed in this study are those of the author
and are not to be taken as reflecting the views of UNESCO

First published in Great Britain in 1997 by the Institute of Art and Law,
Bank Chambers, 121 London Road, Leicester, LE2 0~~~~~~
Tel: 0116 255 5146; fax: 0116 255 1782; e-mail: ial@pipemedia.co.uk

The author is currently Chief of the International Standards Section in the Division of Cultural
Heritage of UNESCO, Paris. Until 1996, she was Professor of Cultural Heritage Law at the
University of Sydney.

Cover design: James Redmond-Cooper

The cover design is based on a bronze statuette from Gandhara in Pakistan. The region is renowned
for small figures of the Buddha or Boddisattvas of very high artistic quality and with unique
stylistic features developed in the 8th to 9th centuries A.D. They are in high demand in the
international art market and in 1995 the National Museum of Pakistan advertised ten missing
items and sought public help to recover them. Subsequently six of them were found.

ISBN: 0 9531696 0 X

Typeset by Keith Marriott, Institute of Art and Law.

DEDICATION

In memory of Malcolm Evans
Secretary-general of UNIDROIT 1984-1997

whose inspired leadership ensured the success
of efforts to achieve the Convention

TABLE OF CONTENTS

TABLE OF CASES

UNIDROIT CONVENTION ON STOLEN OR ILLEGALLY EXPORTED CULTURAL OBJECTS

THE STATES PARTIES TO THIS CONVENTION,

ASSEMBLED in Rome at the invitation of the Government of the Italian Republic from 7 to 24 June 1995 for a Diplomatic Conference for the adoption of the draft Unidroit Convention on the International Return of Stolen or Illegally Exported Cultural Objects,

CONVINCED of the fundamental importance of the protection of cultural heritage and of cultural exchanges for promoting understanding between peoples, and the dissemination of culture for the well-being of humanity and the progress of civilisation,

DEEPLY CONCERNED by the illicit trade in cultural objects and the irreparable damage frequently caused by it, both to these objects themselves and to the cultural heritage of national, tribal, indigenous or other communities, and also to the heritage of all peoples, and in particular by the pillage of archaeological sites and the resulting loss of irreplaceable archaeological, historical and scientific information,

DETERMINED to contribute effectively to the fight against illicit trade in cultural objects by taking the important step of establishing common, minimal legal rules for the restitution and return of cultural objects between Contracting States, with the objective of improving the preservation and protection of the cultural heritage in the interest of all,

EMPHASISING that this Convention is intended to facilitate the restitution and return of cultural objects, and that the provision of any remedies, such as compensation, needed to effect restitution and return in some States, does not imply that such remedies should be adopted in other States,

AFFIRMING that the adoption of the provisions of this Convention for the future in no way confers any approval or legitimacy upon illegal transactions of whatever kind which may have taken place before the entry into force of the Convention,

CONSCIOUS that this Convention will not by itself provide a solution to the problems raised by illicit trade, but that it initiates a process that will enhance international cultural co-operation and maintain a proper role for legal trading and inter-State agreements for cultural exchanges,

ACKNOWLEDGING that implementation of this Convention should be accompanied by other effective measures for protecting cultural objects, such as the development and use of registers, the physical protection of archaeological sites and technical co-operation,

RECOGNISING the work of various bodies to protect cultural property, particularly the 1970 UNESCO Convention on illicit traffic and the development of codes of conduct in the private sector,

HAVE AGREED as follows:

CHAPTER I — SCOPE OF APPLICATION AND DEFINITION

Article 1

This Convention applies to claims of an international character for:

(a)   the restitution of stolen cultural objects;

(b)   the return of cultural objects removed from the territory of a Contracting State contrary to its law regulating the export of cultural objects for the purpose of protecting its cultural heritage (hereinafter "illegally exported cultural objects").

Article 2

For the purposes of this Convention, cultural objects are those which, on religious or secular grounds, are of importance for archaeology, prehistory, history, literature, art or science and belong to one of the categories listed in the Annex to this Convention.

CHAPTER II — RESTITUTION OF STOLEN CULTURAL OBJECTS

Article 3

(1)   The possessor of a cultural object which has been stolen shall return it.

(2)   For the purposes of this Convention, a cultural object which has been unlawfully excavated or lawfully excavated but unlawfully retained shall be considered stolen, when consistent with the law of the State where the excavation took place.

(3)   Any claim for restitution shall be brought within a period of three years from the time when the claimant knew the location of the cultural object and the identity of its possessor, and in any case within a period of fifty years from the time of the theft.

(4)   However, a claim for restitution of a cultural object forming an integral part of an identified monument or archaeological site, or belonging to a public collection, shall not be subject to time limitations other than a period of three years from the time when the claimant knew the location of the cultural object and the identity of its possessor.

(5)   Notwithstanding the provisions of the preceding paragraph, any Contracting State may declare that a claim is subject to a time limitation of 75 years or such longer period as is provided in its law. A claim made in another Contracting State for restitution of a cultural object displaced from a monument, archaeological site or public collection in a Contracting State making such a declaration shall also be subject to that time limitation.

(6)   A declaration referred to in the preceding paragraph shall be made at the time of signature, ratification, acceptance, approval or accession.

(7)   For the purposes of this Convention, a "public collection" consists of a group of inventoried or otherwise identified cultural objects owned by:

(a)   a Contracting State

(b)   a regional or local authority of a Contracting State;

(c)   a religious institution in a Contracting State; or

(d)   an institution that is established for an essentially cultural, educational or scientific purpose in a Contracting State and is recognized in that State as serving the public interest.

(8)   In addition, a claim for restitution of a sacred or communally important cultural object belonging to and used by a tribal or indigenous community in a Contracting State as part of that community's traditional or ritual use, shall be subject to the time limitation applicable to public collections.

Article 4

(1)   The possessor of a stolen cultural object required to return it shall be entitled, at the time of its restitution, to payment of fair and reasonable compensation provided that the possessor neither knew nor ought reasonably to have known that the object was stolen and can prove that it exercised due diligence when acquiring the object.

(2)   Without prejudice to the right of the possessor to compensation referred to in the preceding paragraph, reasonable efforts shall be made to have the person who transferred the cultural object to the possessor, or any prior transferor, pay the compensation where to do so would be consistent with the law of the State in which the claim is brought.

(3)   Payment of compensation to the possessor by the claimant, when this is required, shall be without prejudice to the right of the claimant to recover it from any other person.

(4)   In determining whether the possessor exercised due diligence, regard shall be had to all the circumstances of the acquisition, including the character of the parties, the price paid, whether the possessor consulted any reasonably accessible register of stolen cultural objects, and any other relevant information and documentation which it could reasonably have obtained, and whether the possessor consulted accessible agencies or took any other step that a reasonable person would have taken in the circumstances.

(5)   The possessor shall not be in a more favourable position than the person from whom it acquired the cultural object by inheritance or otherwise gratuitously.

CHAPTER III — RETURN OF ILLEGALLY EXPORTED CULTURAL OBJECTS

Article 5

(1)   A Contracting State may request the court or other competent authority of another Contracting State to order the return of a cultural object illegally exported from the territory of the requesting State.

(2)   A cultural object which has been temporarily exported from the territory of the requesting State, for purposes such as exhibition, research or restoration, under a permit issued according to its law regulating its export for the purpose of protecting its cultural heritage and not returned in accordance with the terms of that permit shall be deemed to have been illegally exported.

(3)   The court or other competent authority of the State addressed shall order the return of an illegally exported cultural object if the requesting State establishes that the removal of the object from its territory significantly impairs one or more of the following interests:

(a)   the physical preservation of the object or its context;

(b)   the integrity of a complex object;

(c)   the preservation of information of, for example, a scientific or historical character;

(d)   the traditional or ritual use of the object by a tribal or indigenous community,

or establishes that the object is of significant cultural importance for the requesting State.

(4)   Any request made under paragraph 1 of this article shall contain or be accompanied by such information of a factual or legal nature as may assist the court or other competent authority of the State addressed in determining whether the requirements of paragraphs 1 to 3 have been met.

(5)   Any request for return shall be brought within a period of three years from the time when the requesting State knew the location of the cultural object and the identity of its possessor, and in any case within a period of fifty years from the date of the export or from the date on which the object should have been returned under a permit referred to in paragraph 2 of this article.

Article 6

(1)   The possessor of a cultural object who acquired the object after it was illegally exported shall be entitled, at the time of its return, to payment by the requesting State of fair and reasonable compensation, provided that the possessor neither knew nor ought reasonably to have known at the time of

acquisition that the object had been illegally exported.

(2)　In determining whether the possessor knew or ought reasonably to have known that the cultural object had been illegally exported, regard shall be had to the circumstances of the acquisition, including the absence of an export certificate required under the law of the requesting State.

(3)　Instead of compensation, and in agreement with the requesting State, the possessor required to return the cultural object to that State, may decide:

    (a)　to retain ownership of the object; or

    (b)　to transfer ownership against payment or gratuitously to a person of its choice residing in the requesting State who provides the necessary guarantees.

(4)　The cost of returning the cultural object in accordance with this article shall be borne by the requesting State, without prejudice to the right of that State to recover costs from any other person.

(5)　The possessor shall not be in a more favourable position than the person from whom it acquired the cultural object by inheritance or otherwise gratuitously.

Article 7

(1)　The provisions of this Chapter shall not apply where:

    (a)　the export of a cultural object is no longer illegal at the time at which the return is requested; or

    (b)　the object was exported during the lifetime of the person who created it or within a period of fifty years following the death of that person.

(2)　Notwithstanding the provisions of sub-paragraph (b) of the preceding paragraph, the provisions of this Chapter shall apply where a cultural object was made by a member or members of a tribal or indigenous community for traditional or ritual use by that community and the object will be returned to that community.

CHAPTER IV — GENERAL PROVISIONS

Article 8

(1)　A claim under Chapter II and a request under Chapter III may be brought before the courts or other competent authorities of the Contracting State where the cultural object is located, in addition to the courts or other competent authorities otherwise having jurisdiction under the rules in force in Contracting States.

(2)　The parties may agree to submit the dispute to any court or other competent authority or to arbitration.

(3)   Resort may be had to the provisional, including protective, measures available under the law of the Contracting State where the object is located even when the claim for restitution or request for return of the object is brought before the courts or other competent authorities of another Contracting State.

Article 9

(1)   Nothing in this Convention shall prevent a Contracting State from applying any rules more favourable to the restitution or the return of stolen or illegally exported cultural objects than provided for by this Convention.

(2)   This article shall not be interpreted as creating an obligation to recognise or enforce a decision of a court or other competent authority of another Contracting State that departs from the provisions of this Convention.

Article 10

(1)   The provisions of Chapter II shall apply only in respect of a cultural object that is stolen after this Convention enters into force in respect of the State where the claim is brought, provided that:

   (a)   the object was stolen from the territory of a Contracting State after the entry into force of this Convention for that State; or

   (b)   the object is located in a Contracting State after the entry into force of the Convention for that State.

(2)   The provisions of Chapter III shall apply only in respect of a cultural object that is illegally exported after this Convention enters into force for the requesting State as well as the State where the request is brought.

(3)   This Convention does not in any way legitimise any illegal transaction of whatever nature which has taken place before the entry into force of this Convention or which is excluded under paragraphs (1) or (2) of this article, nor limit any right of a State or other person to make a claim under remedies available outside the framework of this Convention for the restitution or return of a cultural object stolen or illegally exported before the entry into force of this Convention.

CHAPTER V — FINAL PROVISIONS

Article 11

(1)   This Convention is open for signature at the concluding meeting of the Diplomatic Conference for the adoption of the draft Unidroit Convention on the International Return of Stolen or Illegally Exported Cultural Objects and will remain open for signature by all States at Rome until 30 June 1996.

(2)   This Convention is subject to ratification, acceptance or approval by States which have signed it.

(3)   This Convention is open for accession by all States which are not signatory States as from the date it is open for signature.

(4)   Ratification, acceptance, approval or accession is subject to the deposit of a formal instrument to that effect with the depositary.

Article 12

(1)   This Convention shall enter into force on the first day of the sixth month following the date of deposit of the fifth instrument of ratification, acceptance, approval or accession.

(2)   For each State that ratifies, accepts, approves or accedes to this Convention after the deposit of the fifth instrument of ratification, acceptance, approval or accession, this Convention shall enter into force in respect of that State on the first day of the sixth month following the date of deposit of its instrument of ratification, acceptance, approval or accession.

Article 13

(1)   This Convention does not affect any international instrument by which any Contracting State is legally bound and which contains provisions on matters governed by this Convention, unless a contrary declaration is made by the States bound by such instrument.

(2)   Any Contracting State may enter into agreements with one or more Contracting States, with a view to improving the application of this Convention in their mutual relations. The States which have concluded such an agreement shall transmit a copy to the depositary.

(3)   In their relations with each other, Contracting States which are Members of organisations of economic integration or regional bodies may declare that they will apply the internal rules of these organisations or bodies and will not therefore apply as between these States the provisions of this Convention the scope of application of which coincides with that of those rules.

Article 14

(1)   If a Contracting State has two or more territorial units, whether or not possessing different systems of law applicable in relation to the matters dealt with in this Convention, it may, at the time of signature or of the deposit of its instrument of ratification, acceptance, approval or accession, declare that this Convention is to extend to all its territorial units or only to one or more of them, and may substitute for its declaration another declaration at any time.

(2)   These declarations are to be notified to the depositary and are to state expressly the territorial units to which the Convention extends.

(3)   If, by virtue of a declaration under this article, this Convention extends to one or more but not all of the territorial units of a Contracting State, the reference to:

(a)   the territory of a Contracting State in Article 1 shall be construed as referring to the territory of a territorial unit of that State;

(b)   a court or other competent authority of the Contracting State or of the State addressed shall be construed as referring to the court or other competent authority of a territorial unit of that State;

(c)   the Contracting State where the cultural object is located in Article 8 (1) shall be construed as referring to the territorial unit of that State where the object is located;

(d)   the law of the Contracting State where the object is located in Article 8 (3) shall be construed as referring to the law of the territorial unit of that State where the object is located; and

(e)   a Contracting State in Article 9 shall be construed as referring to a territorial unit of that State.

(4)   If a Contracting State makes no declaration under paragraph 1 of this article, this Convention is to extend to all territorial units of that State.

Article 15

(1)   Declarations made under this Convention at the time of signature are subject to confirmation upon ratification, acceptance or approval.

(2)   Declarations and confirmations of declarations are to be in writing and to be formally notified to the depositary.

(3)   A declaration shall take effect simultaneously with the entry into force of this Convention in respect of the State concerned. However, a declaration of which the depositary receives formal notification after such entry into force shall take effect on the first day of the sixth month following the date of its deposit with the depositary.
(4)   Any State which makes a declaration under this Convention may withdraw it at any time by a formal notification in writing addressed to the depositary. Such withdrawal shall take effect on the first day of the sixth month following the date of the deposit of the notification.

Article 16

(1)   Each Contracting State shall at the time of signature, ratification, acceptance, approval or accession, declare that claims for the restitution, or requests for the return, of cultural objects brought by a State under Article 8 may be submitted to it under one or more of the following procedures:

(a)   directly to the courts or other competent authorities of the declaring State;

(b)   through an authority or authorities designated by that State to receive such claims or requests and to forward them to the courts or other competent authorities of that State;

(c)   through diplomatic or consular channels.

(2)   Each Contracting State may also designate the courts or other authorities competent to order the restitution or return of cultural objects under the provisions of Chapters II and III.

(3)   Declarations made under paragraphs 1 and 2 of this article may be modified at any time by a new declaration.

(4)   The provisions of paragraphs 1 to 3 of this article do not affect bilateral or multilateral agreements on judicial assistance in respect of civil and commercial matters that may exist between Contracting States.

Article 17

Each Contracting State shall, no later than six months following the date of deposit of its instrument of ratification, acceptance, approval or accession, provide the depositary with written information in one of the official languages of the Convention concerning the legislation regulating the export of its cultural objects. This information shall be updated from time to time as appropriate.

Article 18

No reservations are permitted except those expressly authorised in this Convention.

Article 19

(1)   This Convention may be denounced by any State Party, at any time after the date on which it enters into force for that State, by the deposit of an instrument to that effect with the depositary.
(2)   A denunciation shall take effect on the first day of the sixth month following the deposit of the instrument of denunciation with the depositary. Where a longer period for the denunciation to take effect is specified in the instrument of denunciation it shall take effect upon the expiration of such longer period after its deposit with the depositary.

(3)   Notwithstanding such a denunciation, this Convention shall nevertheless apply to a claim for restitution or a request for return of a cultural object submitted prior to the date on which the denunciation takes effect.

Article 20

The President of the International Institute for the Unification of Private Law (Unidroit) may at regular intervals, or at any time at the request of five Contracting States, convene a special committee in order to review the practical operation of this Convention.

Article 21

(1)   This Convention shall be deposited with the Government of the Italian Republic.

(2)   The Government of the Italian Republic shall:

    (a)   inform all States which have signed or acceded to this Convention and the President of the International Institute for the Unification of Private Law (Unidroit) of:

        (i)   each new signature or deposit of an instrument of ratification, acceptance, approval or accession, together with the date thereof;

        (ii)   each declaration made in accordance with this Convention;

        (iii)   the withdrawal of any declaration;

        (iv)   the date of entry into force of this Convention;

        (v)   the agreements referred to in Article 13;

        (vi)   the deposit of an instrument of denunciation of this Convention together with the date of its deposit and the date on which it takes effect;

    (b)   transmit certified true copies of this Convention to all signatory States, to all States acceding to the Convention and to the President of the International Institute for the Unification for Private Law (Unidroit);

    (c)   perform such other functions customary for depositaries.

IN WITNESS WHEREOF the undersigned plenipotentiaries, being duly authorised, have signed this Convention.

DONE at Rome, this twenty-fourth day of June, one thousand nine hundred and ninety-five, in a single original, in the English and French languages, both texts being equally authentic.

ANNEX I

(a)   Rare collections and specimens of fauna, flora, minerals and anatomy, and objects of palaeontological interest;

(b)   property relating to history, including the history of science and technology and military and social history, to the life of national leaders, thinkers, scientists and artists and to events of national importance;

(c)   products of archaeological excavations (including regular and clandestine) or of archaeological discoveries;

(d)   elements of artistic or historical monuments or archaeological sites which have been dismembered;

(e)   antiquities more than one hundred years old, such as inscriptions, coins and engraved seals;

(f)   objects of ethnological interest;

(g)   property of artistic interest, such as:

   (i)   pictures, paintings and drawings produced entirely by hand on any support and in any material (excluding industrial designs and manufactured articles decorated by hand);
   (ii)   original works of statuary art and sculpture in any material;
   (iii)   original engravings, prints and lithographs;
   (iv)   original artistic assemblages and montages in any material;

(h)   rare manuscripts and incunabula, old books, documents and publications of special interest (historical, artistic, scientific, literary, etc.) singly or in collections;

(i)   postage, revenue and similar stamps, singly or in collections;

(j)   archives, including sound, photographic and cinematographic archives;

(k)   articles of furniture more than one hundred years old and old musical instruments.

INTRODUCTION

The adoption on 24 June 1995 of the UNIDROIT Convention on Stolen and Illegally Exported Cultural Objects at the Diplomatic Conference held in Rome was the end of a long process[1]. A report to UNESCO on national legal control of illicit traffic in cultural property in 1982 recommended that UNESCO take up this issue with an international body specialised in private law[2]. The report incorporated earlier suggestions of Professors Chatelain[3] and Rodotà[4] to re-examine the principle of the protection of the *bona fide* purchaser which was seen by these experts as assisting the entry into the licit trade of illicitly traded cultural property. UNESCO commissioned UNIDROIT with this task.

Following two expert studies on the topic[5], UNIDROIT put together a group of experts to draft a preliminary text[6]. After three meetings the text which they produced was ready to go to meetings of Governmental Experts who met four times. As one of the members of the initial group who was also present as Observer for UNESCO at the later meetings, it was interesting to this writer to see the evolution of the draft. It is fair to say that all the arguments which were made in the meetings of Governmental Experts and the Diplomatic Conference, or those which have been made since the adoption of the text, were already rehearsed before the Study Group of Experts who were well aware, not only of the relevant rules of public international law, private international law, trade law, the UNESCO Convention on the Means of Prohibiting and Preventing the Illicit Import, Export and Transfer of Ownership of Cultural Property 1970 and other relevant legal rules, but between them covered the gamut of different legal systems and philosophies. They

---

1. Note on documents: UNIDROIT documents for each of the meetings of the Study Group and group of Governmental Experts, are cited in this article as "Doc. 00". The Acts and Proceedings of the Diplomatic Conference, also published by UNIDROIT, are cited as "Acts". The documents referred to are listed in detail in Appendix I.
2. Prott, L.V. & O'Keefe, P.J. *National Legal Control of Illicit Traffic in Cultural Property* commissioned by UNESCO and discussed at a Consultation of Experts on Illicit Traffic, Paris, 1-4 March 1983, UNESCO Doc. CLT/83/WS/16 (UNESCO, Paris) 1983.
3. Chatelain, J. "Means of Combatting the Theft of and Illegal Traffic in Works of Art in the Nine Countries of the EEC" (Commission of the European Communities, Doc. XII/920/79-E (1976).
4. Rodotà. S., "The Civil Law Aspects of the International Protection of Cultural Property" in Council of Europe, *International Legal Protection of Cultural Property* (1984) 99; "Explanatory Memorandum" in Council of Europe, *The Art Trade* (1988) 1.
5. Reichelt, G. "International Protection of Cultural Property" (1985) *Uniform Law Review*, 43; "The International Protection of Cultural Property: Second Study" (UNIDROIT, Rome) 1988.
6. The Study Group included the following experts: Riccardo Monaco (President of UNIDROIT), Joseph Bayo Ajala (Solicitor-General of Nigeria), Jean Chatelain (former legal counsel of the Musées de France), Richard Crewdson (Solicitor, U.K.), Ridha Fraoua (Consultant to UNESCO, Tunisia/Switzerland), Manlio Frigo (Legal practitioner, Italy), Pierre Lalive d'Epinay (Professor of Law/Legal practitioner, Switzerland), Roland Loewe (former Director-General of the Austrian Federal Department of Justice), John Merryman (Professor at Stanford University, U.S.A.), Aldo Pezzana Capranica del Grillo (Sovereign Order of Malta), Lyndel Prott (Consultant to UNESCO, Australia), Stefano Rodotà (Professor at Rome University), Jorge Sanchez Cordero (Legal practitioner, Mexico), Jelena Vilnius (Professor of Comparative Law, Belgrade), Pieter van Nuffel (European Commission), Georges Droz (Secretary-General of the Hague Conference of Private International Law), Etienne Clément (UNESCO), Régis Brillat (Council of Europe), Elisabeth Gammes (INTERPOL), Gerte Reichelt (Consultant to UNIDROIT, Austria) (not all were present at all meetings). A number of these were specialist writers in the law concerning cultural property (Chatelain, Fraoua, Frigo, Merryman, Prott), others were specialists in private international law (Droz, Lalive) and yet others were lawyers handling cultural property matters for collectors or dealers (Crewdson, Sanchez Cordero) in their respective national legal systems.

were also fully conscious of the various national interests and the points of view of cultural specialists, dealers and collectors. It was notable that, although all of the provisions proposed by the Study Group were re-examined in detail, and many alternative proposals made, the final text adopted bears marked resemblance to that which emerged from the hands of the Study Group. And it is also noteworthy, as stated by the Chairman of the meetings of the Governmental Experts, that, despite many statements applauding the principle of protection but deploring the means adopted by the UNIDROIT Convention to put it into effect, no-one, in the ten years of active negotiation, proposed any other method[7].

Negotiations were not easy. Over 70 States took part at some stage or other of the process (Appendix V). Everyone is aware of the different interests and the emotional nature of the issues ("free trade", "protection of the heritage") in many States. Although all the issues and arguments were aired in the Study Group, the strength of the feelings involved in many national populations, and the evident need of many delegates to meet the demands of home constituencies, were most evident at the four meetings of Governmental Experts. At the Diplomatic Conference there was a majority of States who had major problems of illicit export over those which had important art markets. Votes had often been very close in the experts' meetings. At the Diplomatic Conference issue after issue was decided by vote favouring the positions of the "exporting" States. Delegations from some Western countries, concerned at the possible adoption of a text which they knew would have virtually no chance of acceptance in their States, were expressing concern.

In the third (and last) week of the discussions the Mexican Delegation took a key role in setting up a "working group" made up of representatives of both "exporting" and "importing" States, and some others, to try to reach some acceptable compromise on certain key provisions such as limitations, the description of illegally exported cultural objects to be returned and the non-retroactivity clause.

For the last four days left in the conference timetable the working group worked intensively to achieve a text which would meet the essential conditions of both sides[8]. That text was finally ready late on the last day of the conference and was adopted by the Plenum in preference to that voted by the Committee of the Whole earlier that day[9].

Such a history is, of course, not unusual in the annals of international conferences[10]. The fact that the Convention was adopted shows, in fact, the strong commitment that all States present had to achieving a text that would be satisfactory for as many of the participating States as possible. The Convention was adopted by thirty-five affirmative, five negative votes and seventeen abstentions.

---

7. Lalive, P. "Une Avancée du Droit international: la Convention de Rome d'UNIDROIT sur les Biens culturels volés ou illicitement exportés" 1 *Uniform Law Review* (1996) 57.
8. The working group first included Egypt, France, Greece, Iran, Ireland, Italy, Mexico, the Republic of Korea, Spain, Turkey, the United States, Zambia and at a late stage was joined by Australia and Canada. Its meetings appear to have been stormy: the Netherlands and Switzerland retired from it at one stage but were able to join in the compromise text submitted to the Plenary Session; Egypt, on the other hand, did not, and was one of the only five delegations voting against the text finally adopted which included these compromise articles. At the final plenary session Cambodia, Ireland, Korea and Zambia joined as "original authors". The Secretariat was not present during these essentially political meetings and the draft was presented to the Plenary meeting without detailed explanation of the changes. This is unfortunate, since there are some questions on which a record of the views of those participating in reaching the drafting concerned would have been very useful for the interpretation of the Convention. See, for example, the commentary on Art. 10(1).
9. Acts 356-358.
10. For an account of the proceedings of the Diplomatic Conference by a participant attending one for the first time, see Crewdson, R. "On the Making of Conventions" 21 *International Legal Practitioner* (1996) 89-92.

It is clear that, despite the difficult negotiations, there was substantial consensus for the text: the five negative votes were a procedural protest rather than a vote on the substance[11] and many of the abstentions were due to the impossibility of getting approval of the new text from capitals in time for signature[12].

Twenty-two States signed the Convention[13] before 30 June 1996, after which it was no longer open for signature, and three States have become party[14] (up to July 1997). It seems appropriate, now that the Convention is on its way to ratification and entry into force (which requires only five States party), to give a brief commentary on its historical evolution and the interpretation of its various articles.

---

11. Egypt and four other Arab States, Acts 359 (Hawas).
12. There is no official list of the voting as it was taken on a show of hands and not a roll call.
13. Burkina Faso, Bolivia, Cambodia, Côte d'Ivoire, Croatia, Finland, France, Georgia, Guinea, Hungary, Italy, Lithuania, Netherlands, Pakistan, Paraguay, Peru, Portugal, Romania, Russian Federation, Senegal, Switzerland and Zambia.
14. China, Lithuania and Paraguay.

RELATIONSHIP TO THE UNESCO CONVENTION

One question that immediately arises is the relationship of this new Convention to the UNESCO Convention[1]. As UNESCO was at the origin of this work, it naturally took a very close interest in its progress and was represented at all stages of the negotiations. The links between the two Conventions are evident, especially in the definition section. The UNESCO Convention deals with the problem of illicit traffic by means of administrative procedures and State action; the UNIDROIT Convention provides direct access to the courts of one State by the owner of a stolen cultural object or by a State from which it has been illicitly exported. They thus complement one another.

However it should also be evident how much the 1995 Convention has benefited from the advance in public attitudes towards illicit traffic in the 25 years since the adoption of the UNESCO Convention. The UNIDROIT Convention applies to all stolen cultural objects whereas Article 7 of the UNESCO Convention has been interpreted as restricting the obligation of return only to objects inventoried in institutions. The UNIDROIT Convention has also developed a sophisticated way of dealing with the differences between legal systems on protection of a "good faith" acquirer.

In this respect the UNESCO Convention has been a path setter and has enabled governments and concerned citizens to keep the issue of illicit traffic before the public. It has also inspired Codes of Ethics, such as that of the International Council of Museums (ICOM) and the British Code of Practice which, valuable in themselves, are also forerunners of more effective legislative action now seen as acceptable and necessary to States which have previously been reluctant to accept the obligations of the 1970 Convention.

---

1. Fraoua, R. "Le projet de convention de l'UNIDROIT sur le retour international des biens culturels volés ou illicitement exportés" *Aktuelle Juristische Praxis 3/1995 317* at 325-326; Prott, L.V. "UNESCO and UNIDROIT: a Partnership against Illicit Trafficking" 1 *Uniform Law Review* (1996) 59-71.

GENERAL ISSUES

At the very beginning of the project it was not decided by the Study Group whether the rules would be embodied in an International Convention or a model law[1]. As the exercise progressed it became more and more clear that minimal rules had to be negotiated and that the acceptance of certain rules by some States depended on the acceptance of other rules by other participants. It became obvious that an international Convention was the best way to proceed. The final text of the Convention prevents reservations — fears that true reciprocity would otherwise be lost played a part in that decision (see discussion on Article 18).

One question which had to be decided was whether the new rules as to the return of cultural property should apply to all transactions, domestic and international, or only those involved in international commerce. The first meeting of the Study Group of Experts had before it a preliminary draft prepared by Roland Loewe of Austria who had chosen the first solution[2]. Some delegations expressed their discomfort with this view[3] and at the second meeting of Governmental Experts a consensus emerged to deal only with international transactions[4]. This was unfortunate in one respect, in that it prevented the development of a more uniform set of rules and there was a strong feeling on the part of some experts that the Convention should apply to purely domestic transactions as well, not least because of the difficulty of deciding when a transaction was national and when it was international[5]. Although ultimately Article 1(a) refers to "claims of an international character", one expert in private international law has expressed the view that, based on experience with other international conventions on private law, the effect would not be much different, since governments would rapidly find it impossible in such circumstances to maintain a position which is less favourable to their own citizen-owners than to those of other countries.

It is important to note that, although participants and commentators (including this one), speak of "importing" and "exporting" States, this is a kind of rudimentary shorthand for a much more complex problem. Although current trade flows may render a country likely to see itself as one or the other, this can change at any time. It is also true that even the most developed countries with a highly professional and alert cultural bureaucracy cannot prevent clandestine excavation and theft (France, United Kingdom and United States, to cite just three). Some States see themselves as both, and some States are really "transit" States with a far bigger through traffic of cultural objects than either definitive import or export. There was, therefore, and is, a substantial concurrence of interest, shown by the pattern of final voting, of *all* States to achieve an instrument which would provide a better means of international legal collaboration than exists at present.

---

1. Doc. 10 § 10. The Commonwealth of English-speaking countries has chosen to prepare a draft model law for the implementation of its "Scheme for the Protection of Cultural Heritage within the Commonwealth" adopted Mauritius, November 1993 (Commonwealth Secretariat, London). The draft model law will is still under consideration. Text of the Scheme is given in Appendix VIII.
2. Doc. 10 § 30; Doc. 18 § 24.
3. Doc. 23 §§ 12, 33-34; Doc. 30 §§ 41-42, 9.
4. Doc. 23 §§ 17, 152; 30 §§ 10-17, 23.
5. Doc. 30 §§ 12-15; cf. Siehr, K. "Vereinheitlichung des Mobiliarsachenrechts in Europa, insbesondere im Hinblick auf Kulturgüter" 59 *Rabels Zeitschrift für ausländisches und internationales Privatrecht* (1995) 454 at 463. See also discussion on Article 1.

TITLE

UNIDROIT CONVENTION ON STOLEN OR ILLEGALLY EXPORTED CULTURAL OBJECTS

The title to the Convention was discussed with care, and the divisions of opinion which appeared were already an indicator of the divergent views on the value and purpose of the Convention.

At an early stage a member of the Study Group objected to the title "Convention for the Protection of Cultural Property", on the ground that ensuring the recovery of cultural objects did not necessarily involve protection. Others found it perfectly satisfactory and supported by national legislative practice[1]. Another expert disliked the word "property" which, at any rate in English, had connotations which could be misleading[2], and proposed the used of the word "heritage". This was challenged as "emotive" language, and ultimately the compromise "cultural objects" was accepted (the French term *biens culturels* remaining unchanged)[3].

Another discussion took place on the possible insertion of the words "restitution and return of"[4]. The third meeting of experts approved "Draft Convention on Stolen or Illegally Exported Cultural Objects". However the text submitted to the Diplomatic Conference by the fourth meeting of Governmental Experts was "Draft Convention on the International Return of Stolen or Illegally Exported Cultural Objects"[5]. The Diplomatic Conference returned to the shorter form[6]. It was difficult to find an accurate rendering in both languages of "restitution" since it does not mean the same in French law as in English, and the use of the terms "restitution" and "return" in UNESCO practice[7] was different again. Although some delegations wanted the concept of "international restitution" in the title, to indicate that the Convention would not necessarily be applied in purely domestic situations, it was finally decided to deal with this in the text of the Convention (see now Art. 1) and not in the title.

---

1. Doc. 10 §§ 7-9.
2. Prott, L.V. & O'Keefe, P.J. "'Cultural heritage' or 'Cultural property'?" 1 *International Journal of Cultural Property* (1992) 307.
3. Doc. 10 § 9; Doc. 18 § 20; Doc. 30 § 21.
4. Doc. 14 § 9; Doc. 18 §§ 16-20.
5 Doc. 48 § 14.
6. Acts 155, 277.
7. E.g. by the UNESCO Intergovernmental Committee for Promoting the Return of Cultural Property to Its Countries of Origin or Its Restitution in Case of Illicit Appropriation.

THE PREAMBLE

THE STATES PARTIES TO THIS CONVENTION,

ASSEMBLED in Rome at the invitation of the Government of the Italian Republic from 7 to 24 June 1995 for a Diplomatic Conference for the adoption of the draft Unidroit Convention on the International Return of Stolen or Illegally Exported Cultural Objects,

CONVINCED of the fundamental importance of the protection of cultural heritage and of cultural exchanges for promoting understanding between peoples, and the dissemination of culture for the well-being of humanity and the progress of civilisation,

DEEPLY CONCERNED by the illicit trade in cultural objects and the irreparable damage frequently caused by it, both to these objects themselves and to the cultural heritage of national, tribal, indigenous or other communities, and also to the heritage of all peoples, and in particular by the pillage of archaeological sites and the resulting loss of irreplaceable archaeological, historical and scientific information,

DETERMINED to contribute effectively to the fight against illicit trade in cultural objects by taking the important step of establishing common, minimal legal rules for the restitution and return of cultural objects between Contracting States, with the objective of improving the preservation and protection of the cultural heritage in the interest of all,

EMPHASISING that this Convention is intended to facilitate the restitution and return of cultural objects, and that the provision of any remedies, such as compensation, needed to effect restitution and return in some States, does not imply that such remedies should be adopted in other States,

AFFIRMING that the adoption of the provisions of this Convention for the future in no way confers any approval or legitimacy upon illegal transactions of whatever kind which may have taken place before the entry into force of the Convention,

CONSCIOUS that this Convention will not by itself provide a solution to the problems raised by illicit trade, but that it initiates a process that will enhance international cultural co-operation and maintain a proper role for legal trading and inter-State agreements for cultural exchanges,

ACKNOWLEDGING that implementation of this Convention should be accompanied by other effective measures for protecting cultural objects, such as the development and use of registers, the physical protection of archaeological sites and technical co-operation,

RECOGNISING the work of various bodies to protect cultural property, particularly the 1970 UNESCO Convention on illicit traffic and the development of codes of conduct in the private sector,

HAVE AGREED as follows: ...

The Preamble should not be ignored. It is a useful aid in interpretation of the rest of the treaty. The Vienna Convention on the Law of Treaties[1] provides (Art. 31(2)) that a treaty is to be interpreted in good faith in accordance with its context, and context is defined to include its Preamble.

The Preamble was not presented in draft to any of the expert meetings, although proposals were made from time to time to consider the inclusion of one or other element[2]. UNESCO provided a draft Preamble for the fourth meeting of experts and for the Diplomatic Conference[3]. Many of the elements proposed were adopted, though rephrased, in the final version. The Preamble was only briefly discussed at the Diplomatic Conference[4], but was a text elaborated by a group which represented the diverse interests of the delegations — Australia, Canada, France, Greece, Italy, Mexico, Netherlands, Spain, Switzerland, the United States and Zambia[5] — and some elements in it were part of the compromise worked out by the special working group in the last days of the conference.

There are some important inclusions in the Preamble. It specifically mentions the fundamental importance of cultural exchanges for promoting understanding between peoples, and the dissemination of culture (§ 2) and the maintenance of a proper role for legal trading and inter-State agreements for cultural exchanges (§ 7). Statements that the Convention is

> fuelled by the primitive piece of demagogic ideology that all art collectors, dealers and museums in the West are evil, greedy and out to rob poor, defenceless and altruistic countries of their cultural heritage

are simply not responsible[6].

Significantly the Preamble has mentioned the irreparable damage that can be caused by the illicit trade "**to the cultural heritage of national, tribal, indigenous or other communities, and also to the heritage of all peoples**" (§ 2) — in other words, heritage[7] must be considered in its significance for local communities, nations and humanity as a whole. The philosophy of the Convention thus rejects the suggested opposition between "internationalism" (in favour of unrestricted trade) and "retentionism" (national controls on movement) which have been

---

1. 1155 UNTS 331; 63 AJIL (1969) 875; 8 ILM (1969) 679. There are now 81 States Parties to this Convention.
2. Doc. 18 § 8.
3. Acts 89.
4. Acts 333.
5. Acts 355.
6. Feilchenfeldt, W. "I believe in the Future of Collecting . . ." Interview with Christian von Faber-Castell in "TEFAF Basel 96" *Catalogue of the Basel Fine Arts Fair* (1996), 22.
7. A significant contribution to the study of the heritage concept is that of Genius-Devine, B. *Bedeutung und Grenzen des Erbes der Menschheit in völkerrechtlichen Kulturgüterschutz* (Baden-Baden, 1996).

suggested[8]. Since the flow is generally only in favour of the industrialised States, other characterisations have been suggested i.e. that the "free trade" view represents imperialism, and national control real internationalism, since it ensures access to cultural property for those not able to compete with the Western market[9].

Also important is the mention that the aim of the Convention is to achieve

> common, minimal legal rules for the restitution and return of cultural objects between Contracting States, with the objective of improving the preservation and protection of the cultural heritage in the interest of all (§ 4)[10].

A key statement for the interpretation and implementation of the Convention in many States is paragraph 5.

> . . . this Convention is intended to facilitate the restitution and return of cultural objects, and . . . the provision of any remedies, such as compensation, needed to effect restitution and return in some States, does not imply that such remedies should be adopted in other States.

This statement clarifies and strengthens the provisions of Article 9 which encourage a State to retain more favourable rules such as not recognising a change of title to a stolen cultural object and thus not providing for compensation.

Another crucial statement, important to the acceptance of the principle of Article 10 on non-retroactivity and reinforcing it, is the statement (§ 5) that nothing in the Convention confers any approval or legitimacy upon illegal transactions of whatever kind which may have taken place before the entry into force of the Convention[11].

The final paragraph mentions the 1970 UNESCO Convention. On the few occasions where a possible cross-reference to this Convention had been proposed, some States were uneasy because

---

8. A view put by Merryman in a series of articles, see Merryman, J.H. "International Art Law: from Cultural Nationalism to a Common Cultural Heritage" (1983) 15 *New York University Journal of International Law and Politics* 757, "Trading in Art: Cultural Nationalism v. Internationalism" (1984) 18 *Stanford Lawyer* 24; "Two Ways of Thinking about Cultural Property" 80 *American Journal of International Law* 831, "The Retention of Cultural Property" (1988) 21 *University of California Davis Law Review* 477; see the detailed analysis by von Schorlemer, S. of the possible implications of "common heritage" and "national heritage" in *Internationaler Kulturgüterschutz* (Berlin, 1992) 560-583; also commentary by Turner, S. "Cultural Property as National Heritage and Common Human Heritage — The Problem of Reconciling Common and Individual Interests" paper presented to the meeting on "The Penal Protection of Cultural Property" organised by the International Institute of Higher Studies in Criminal Sciences, Siracusa, 22-26 March 1992; Strati, A. "The Implication of Common Heritage Concepts on the Quest for Cultural Objects and the Dialogue between North and South" 89 *ASIL Proceedings* (1995) 439; Müller-Katzenberg, A. *Internationale Standards im Kulturgüterverkehr und ihre Bedeutung für das Sach- und Kollisionsrecht* (Berlin, 1995) 154-157; Genius-Devine, B. book cited last note, 405-407. There was one echo of Merryman's view by a governmental expert who suggested that "very often cultural objects would be better protected if they were exported" Doc. 48 § 106.
9. Vincent, S. "Who Owns Art?" *Art and Auction (U.S.)* 80, 82-83. Mario Chiti, in his presentation to the conference on "Law and Art: the Free Movement of Cultural Property" Maastricht 6-7 March 1997 termed the latter "welfare cosmopolitanism". See also p. 24,nn. 21-23 and related text.
10. The aim of establishing a minimum of uniform rules had been emphasised from the earliest days of the project; Doc. 10 §§ 19, 29, 35; reiterated frequently throughout the negotiations Doc. 18, §§ 133, 135; Doc. 23 § 29, 159-161; Explanatory Report 14; cf. Acts 175.
11. As to the importance of this issue see the discussion of Article 10.

they were not party to this Convention[12]. On the other hand, many other States were, and in view of the careful complementarity of the provisions (including the adoption of the exact categories of material covered by the UNESCO Convention), it seemed unrealistic not to mention it. The compromise reached was to recognise its work in the Preamble without referring to it in the operative part of the Convention. The reference at least excludes any interpretation which would necessarily create an opposition between the two Conventions.

---

12. Doc. 18 § 8.

ARTICLE 1

This article was introduced at the third session of the Expert Study Group[1].

> This Convention applies to claims of an international character for:
>
> (a)   the restitution of stolen cultural objects;

The phrase "**claims of an international character**" was to meet the concern of States who wanted to make it clear that the Convention would not necessarily apply to domestic claims. Strictly speaking, it is redundant in applying to 1(b), since claims for the return from another country of illegally exported objects are necessarily of "an international character"[2].

The phrasing of this article does not make completely clear whether the Convention would apply to a case such as *Winkworth v. Christie Manson and Woods Ltd.*[3] where the cultural objects of an English collector were stolen from him and sold in Italy to an Italian who, some two years after the theft, offered them for sale at Christie's, London. While some Governmental Experts thought that the Convention should not apply in such a situation, there are good reasons to ensure that, where an international transaction has taken place, the Convention should apply, even if the litigation takes place in the first jurisdiction. If it does not, there will be an incentive for dishonest dealers to "launder" goods through any convenient foreign jurisdiction and return the goods with impunity to the jurisdiction where the original owner was deprived of them. The dominant view, with which this writer agrees, is that the UNIDROIT Convention does solve this problem: the result of *Winkworth v. Christie* would be reversed[4]. Does an intervening transaction constitute "a claim of an international character"? The wording of this article, as well as of Article 10 (discussed below), would enable the judge to employ this principle of common sense in keeping with the intention of the Convention[5]. "Laundering" of cultural objects by passage through another country is one of the very problems which the Convention was designed to counter[6].

Article 1(b)

> (b)   the return of cultural objects removed from the territory of a Contracting State contrary to its law regulating the export of cultural objects for the purpose of protecting its cultural heritage (hereinafter "illegally exported cultural objects").

---

1. Doc. 23 §§ 22-23.
2. On the drafting of this phrase and alternative proposals see Doc. 30 §§ 10-17; Doc. 39 §§ 12-20; Doc 48 §§ 12-19; Acts 157-159, 277-278. See also p. 16, nn. 4-6 above.
3. [1980] 1 Ch. 496 [England].
4. Droz, G. "Convention d'UNIDROIT sur les biens volés ou illicitement exportés" forthcoming in *Revue critique de droit international privé* (July 1997) § 15, n. 21; Lalive, art. cited p. 13, n. 7, 57; Siehr, K. art. cited p.16, n. 5, 463. Reichelt, G., takes the contrary view, "Die Rolle von UNIDROIT für den Internationalen Kulturgüterschutz" in *Europa im Aufbruch: Festschrift Fritz Schwind* (1993) 205, 210.
5. Cf. the discussion on this point of Siehr, art. cited p. 16, n. 5, 461-463.
6. This is also the preliminary view of the Law Reform Commission of Ireland in its Consultation Paper, November 1996, 12.

The phrase "**illegally exported**" is defined in Article 1(b) as "**removed from the territory of a contracting State contrary to its law regulating the export of cultural objects for the purpose of protecting its cultural heritage**"[7]. This phrase has been criticised by Merryman[8] on the ground that export regulations are often designed not to "protect" but to "retain" and that works originating outside the State which includes them in export control are not necessarily part of the "heritage" of that State. A more balanced view sees such measures as "protecting" the cultural identity of the human being, in, of course, appropriate balance with legal exchanges of cultural objects[9].

The phrase is the survivor of many other phrases suggested during the course of the negotiations. These included

"contrary to its law applicable to the protection of cultural objects"[10],
"contrary to a legislative provision prohibiting the export of cultural property because of its cultural significance"[11],
"contrary to its legislation"[12],
"contrary to its export legislation"[13],
"contrary to its law"[14],
"contrary to its relevant legislation"[15],
"contrary to its law applicable to the protection of cultural objects[16] and to the disposal of property rights therein"[17],
"contrary to the mandatory rules of law of the State in question"[18],
"contrary to its law regulating the export of cultural objects because of their cultural significance"[19]

and other variations[20].

It can be seen that some of these are extremely narrow in their ambit ("disposal of property rights" or "mandatory rules" — possibly excluding rules on exchanges and loans by museums which are surely relevant), while others were felt to be too wide. Some delegations feared that the text "contrary to its law of export" might include simple customs infractions which had no relevance to the cultural significance of the object and where the cultural value of the object was, as it were, incidental to the breach of the law. Another interpretation was that this might mean that only laws on export (i.e. customs legislation) could be observed, and a foreign court or other competent authority might not apply an export prohibition where it was contained in the relevant cultural heritage legislation.

---

7. Acts 276.
8. Merryman, J.H. "The UNIDROIT Convention: Three Significant Departures from the Urtext" 5 *International Journal of Cultural Property* (1996) 11, 12-13.
9. Fiedler, W. "Vom territorialen zum humanitären Kulturgüterschutz" in Fechner, F., Oppermann, T. & Prott, L.V. *Prinzipien des Kulturgüterschutzes* (Duncker & Humblot, Berlin) 159, 167-171.
10. Doc. 23 § 34; Doc. 30 §§ 19, 26; Doc. 48 § 20.
11. Doc. 23 § 94.
12. Doc. 23 § 30; Doc. 30 §§ 18-19.
13. Doc. 23 §§ 30-31; Doc. 30 §§ 18-20.
14. Doc. 30 § 26.
15. Doc. 30 § 19.
16. Doc. 30 § 19; Doc. 39 § 22; Doc. 48 §§ 20, 191.
17. Doc. 39 § 22.
18. Doc. 39 § 88.
19. Doc. 30, 79; Acts 159.
20. Doc. 30 § 78; Doc. 39 §§ 86-88.

Merryman's suggestion[21] that "protection" and "retention" should be distinguished has not been accepted by other scholars in the subject[22]. A State has a right to at least an adequate representative collection of its national heritage[23] and must, therefore, be able to protect that right. There can, therefore, be no justification for interpreting the Convention by using "protection" in the very narrow sense he has proposed. The term is used throughout the Convention in the broader sense.

Nor has Merryman's suggestion been adopted that objects of foreign origin cannot be accepted as part of the heritage of a State. The UNESCO 1970 Convention Article 4 makes clear that several States may regard an object as part of their heritage: claims are not mutually exclusive, and many States — particularly States of large-scale immigration such as Canada and Australia — do regard important objects originating in other countries with which their populations have significant cultural links as part of their own heritage[24].

The Chinese Delegation proposed "laws and regulations" in this phrase. The Chinese rules of export control 1950-1982 were included in a "Regulation". However the Drafting Committee was quite clear that, both in the English and the French text, the word "law" ("droit") was clearly understood to include regulations[25]. (A somewhat similar terminological question was raised by the Chinese delegation during one of the sessions of the unreported *ad hoc* drafting group set up during one of the latter meetings of the Governmental Experts: did references to a person (e.g. a claimant) include legal as well as physical persons? The consensus was that they were indeed so included.)

Although this definition applies to all cultural objects, the number of *illegally exported* cultural objects affected by the Convention is limited by Article 5(3) (see below) which restricts the ambit of the Convention to illegally exported cultural objects which are of considerable importance to the requesting State.

The phrase "**contrary to its law regulating the export of cultural objects for the purpose of protecting its cultural heritage**" was finally settled in this form at the Diplomatic Conference on the proposal of the Drafting Committee[26].

At the Diplomatic Conference the Croatian Delegation proposed the inclusion of another sub-paragraph which would specifically include cultural objects acquired by armed conflict. The idea was received sympathetically, but the general consensus was that these objects were already covered by the Convention and did not require a special provision[27].

---

21. Merryman, p. 20, n. 8.
22. Doc. 10 §§ 7-8.
23. For a discussion of this principle see O'Keefe, P.J. and Prott, L.V. *Law and the Cultural Heritage: Vol. III - Movement* (Butterworths, London) 1989 864 ff. and note the report of ICOM, *Study on the Principles, Conditions and Means for the Restitution and Return of Cultural Property in view of Reconstituting Dispersed Heritages*, 1977 UNESCO Doc. CC-78/CONF.609/3 Annex 1, also in UNESCO Doc. CC-86/WS/3 Annex 2 and 31 Museum (1979) 62. See also p.20, n. 8 and related text.
24. See also the view of the ICOM Committee on this point, study last cited, § 13.
25. Acts 159.
26. By unanimous vote with only two abstentions, Acts 279.
27. Acts 159-160.

ARTICLE 2

For the purposes of this Convention, cultural objects are those which, on religious or secular grounds, are of importance for archaeology, prehistory, history, literature, art or science and belong to one of the categories listed in the Annex to this Convention.

The Preliminary Draft Convention prepared by the Study Group included the following definition:

> For the purpose of this convention, "cultural object" means any material object of artistic, historical, spiritual, ritual or other cultural significance[1].

This form of definition is characteristic of much national legislation — indeed between 30 and 40 States use such a formula[2]. The Study Group had decided not to adopt a list of the kind used in the UNESCO Convention because it wanted to ensure simplicity[3]. Other versions of a general clause were also considered during the negotiations[4]. However some delegations were suspicious of such a general clause and wanted a more specific definition[5].

At the fourth meeting of Governmental Experts it was agreed to use the same categories as were used in the UNESCO Convention[6], to which 86 States are now party[7]. Various ways of doing this had been discussed in a special working group set up on this matter: some feared that a mere reference to the UNESCO Convention would create problems for anyone for whom the text was not immediately available, or regarded it as unsatisfactory for technical reasons for States which were not party to that Convention to have it partially incorporated in another instrument. The solution reached was to place the categories of the UNESCO definition in an Annex without mentioning the UNESCO Convention (although it is now referred to in the Preamble of the Convention)[8].

Annex

(a) Rare collections and specimens of fauna, flora, minerals and anatomy, and objects of palaeontological interest;

(b) property relating to history, including the history of science and technology and military and social history, to the life of national leaders, thinkers, scientists and artists and to events of national importance;

---

1. Doc. 3, Art. 1. Additional adjectives were suggested Doc. 23 §§ 41-42; Doc. 39 § 34.
2. For a study of the different types of definition used in national legal systems and examples see book cited p.24, n. 23, 26-36.
3. Doc. 14 §§ 11-14.
4. Doc. 18 §§ 25-31; Doc. 23 §§ 35-38; Doc. 30 §§ 27-38; Doc. 39 §§ 25-38; Doc. 48 §§ 37-38.
5. Doc. 23 § 35.
6. First proposed at the second meeting of Governmental Experts, Doc. 30 § 28; Doc. 39 §§ 25-33, 37-38; Doc. 48 §§ 26-46.
7. Listed in Appendix V.
8. Acts §§ 161-165, 279-280.

(c)   products of archaeological excavations (including regular and clandestine) or of archaeological discoveries;

(d)   elements of artistic or historical monuments or archaeological sites which have been dismembered;

(e)   antiquities more than one hundred years old, such as inscriptions, coins and engraved seals;

(f)   objects of ethnological interest;

(g)   property of artistic interest, such as:

     (i)   pictures, paintings and drawings produced entirely by hand on any support and in any material (excluding industrial designs and manufactured articles decorated by hand);
     (ii)   original works of statuary art and sculpture in any material;
     (iii)   original engravings, prints and lithographs;
     (iv)   original artistic assemblages and montages in any material;

(h)   rare manuscripts and incunabula, old books, documents and publications of special interest (historical, artistic, scientific, literary, etc.) singly or in collections;

(i)   postage, revenue and similar stamps, singly or in collections;

(j)   archives, including sound, photographic and cinematographic archives;

(k)   articles of furniture more than one hundred years old and old musical instruments.

There is however a significant departure from the UNESCO formulation: the objects do not have to be "specifically designated by each State" (UNESCO Convention, Art. 1)[9]. For States which designate large amounts of cultural property, such a requirement may be sensible, but there are many States which do not. The United States and the United Kingdom, for example, which do not have the system of classification of movables widely used in the French and similar systems, would find very little of their cultural heritage protected. One of the notable differences in cultural administration is between States which have large amounts of cultural property in State hands and strong State cultural administrations able to administer detailed systems of classification, and those where government ownership of cultural property is the exception rather than the norm and it is rather the interests of private owners which need protection by the Convention.

The UNESCO Convention operates on a State to State level: the UNIDROIT Convention operates on the basis of private law. It is therefore entirely appropriate that cultural objects, whether or not designated, should be covered by the UNIDROIT Convention.

---

9.   This was discussed Doc. 39 §§ 31-32; Doc. 48 §§ 35-37. The text of the Convention can be found in Appendix X.

It has been argued that the definition is too wide[10]. However it must be borne in mind that the full breadth of the definition only applies to stolen, and not to illegally exported cultural objects (see Articles 5 and 7), and that there was a substantial consensus on the importance of covering all stolen cultural objects.

The Loewe preliminary draft contained an article whereby

> cultural property forming part of a collection, set or series or which comes from the same collection, set or series shall be considered to be a single item of property when the same person has been deprived of possession of it or when its export has violated a prohibition, and when it is in the possession of a single person[11].

This article was later dropped. The status of a collection was raised at the Diplomatic Conference[12] but no specific provision on collections was included other than those mentioned in the categories of cultural property listed in the Annex to the Convention[13] and the provisions on public collections in Article 3.

---

10. Acts 161-165, 279-280; Fitzpatrick, J. "Against UNIDROIT" 66 *The Art Newspaper* January 1997 19.
11. Doc. 3 Art. 7(2).
12. Acts 162 (Maroevic), 243 (Khodakov), 297-298.
13. Items (a) and (j).

ARTICLE 3

Perhaps the key Article of the Convention is Article 3.

From the first discussion within the Study Group there was a strong feeling that the issues relating to stolen cultural objects must be distinguished from those applying to objects which were illicitly exported. This approach was endorsed by all subsequent discussion and is probably the reason why the Convention succeeded, since the problem raised in many countries quite distinct legal and philosophical issues. As one delegate to the fourth meeting of Governmental Experts put it,

> In effect, all States were in agreement on the need to co-operate with a view to penalising theft committed abroad as theft was universally considered to be a criminal act, whereas only a few States would, in the present state of the law, be prepared to undertake an obligation to sanction customs offences committed abroad[1].

Article 3(1)

> *The possessor of a cultural object which has been stolen shall return it.*

This provision is of a crystal clarity and imports a significant change in many Civil Law systems[2]. In many cases the only opportunity for a robbed owner to retrieve a unique cultural object from the hands of its purchaser, was to persuade him (there being no legal obligation on him to return it) to sell it back. It will be evident that in such a situation the robbed owner not only had no certainty of persuading the new owner to do so, but was in the worst possible bargaining position. Although within a brief period the robbed owner could insist on return, if the good faith purchaser had bought the goods at auction or through a dealer, compensation would have to be paid (cf. Arts. 2279, 2280 of the French *Civil Code*).

In 1962 UNIDROIT had been entrusted by its Governing Council with the task of drawing up a draft Uniform Law on the protection of the "*bona fide*" purchaser of corporeal movables. The idea was to try and create some uniformity in the rules as to the acquisition of title to movable property. The draft, created by a working committee, was published in 1968. It restricted its scope to international transactions for the sale of goods.

The work was generally favourably received but critical observations were made by governments of the member States of UNIDROIT on the linking of the draft to a project of uniform law on international sale of goods and on over-protection of the "*bona fide*" purchaser. After further work by a Committee of Experts, a revised draft, now known as the draft Uniform Law on the Acquisition in Good Faith of Corporeal Movables (LUAB), was completed in 1974. The starting

---

1. Doc. 48 §§ 52, 100-102, 105-108.
2. Also in English Law, which has departed from the usual Common Law rule that the robbed owner can always recover his or her property by the Limitation Act 1980 which provides that a good faith acquirer is protected after 6 years. See Redmond-Cooper, R. "Limitation Periods in Art Disputes" in *Title and Time in Art and Antiquity Claims* published by the Institute of Art and Law (U.K.) 1995. Although limitation periods apply in all Common Law systems which may limit a robbed owner from recovering the property, generous interpretation of the date from which the limitation period begins in the New York courts has permitted recovery many decades after the theft. See discussion on Article 3(3).

point was no longer to protect first and foremost the transferee in good faith with a view to promoting trade, but rather to look for a fair balance between the interests of the parties concerned: in particular the transferee could in no case invoke his good faith when the goods in question had been stolen. The new draft, however, was not adopted[3].

UNIDROIT's work on the draft 1968-1974 had shown how difficult it would be, in respect of stolen property, to bring about any *rapprochement* between the Common Law jurisdictions which almost unanimously followed the *nemo dat* rule (*nemo dat quod non habet* — no one can transfer what he does not possess i.e. a thief cannot pass title) and most Civil Law systems which, to varying degrees, accorded much wider protection to the *bona fide* purchaser of stolen property[4].

It was clear to the Study Group working on the illicit transfer of cultural objects between 1988 and 1990 that no decision was being made as to the relative moral value of the *nemo dat* rule or that protecting the *bona fide* purchaser. On the one hand it can be argued that the owner had done nothing to deserve the loss of its goods and therefore that the *nemo dat* rule is fair. On the other hand it can be argued that the *bona fide* purchaser has also done nothing to deserve to be deprived of the goods purchased[5].

The absolute duty to return a stolen cultural object was adopted, after much discussion in the first two meetings of the Study Group of Experts[6] at the third meeting of the Study Group[7] in preference to an alternative draft proposal which would have allowed a purchaser who had made prudent inquiries at the time of purchase to be allowed to keep it. One reason expressed was that the former was the only realistic solution which could combat commerce in stolen works of art[8]. A second is that money cannot truly compensate for the loss of a unique cultural object. Consider the loss of unique garden statues from a 400 year old house:

> For . . . me, the priority is to recover these items. . . I am not concerned about receiving insurance money — I don't want any — nor interested in initiating a pastiche replacement. What matters is to recover these particular items historically associated with this place.

> At a more general level it seems reasonably clear that any thief steals for profit in the expectation that he can sell his ill-gotten gains, to a fence or to a final purchaser. . . . In an adult market-place the onus should always be on the purchaser to investigate his title to a possible purchase — *caveat emptor*[9].

The uniqueness of a cultural object is one of the elements which makes them so attractive both to collectors and to thieves and provision for financial compensation to an acquirer may not provide sufficient disincentive to illegal activities.

---

3. Draft Convention providing a uniform law on the acquisition in good faith of corporeal movables with Explanatory Report by J.G. Sauveplanne (UNIDROIT, Rome, Study XLV, Doc. 58) 1975 (known as LUAB, the acronym from Loi uniforme sur l'Acquisition de bonne Foi d'Objets mobiliers corporels). This account is based on Sauveplanne 19-22.
4. Doc. 14 § 25; Explanatory Commentary § 14.
5. The reasoning behind the differing rules on acquisition of movable property in the various systems was analysed by Zweigert, K. "Rechtsvergleichend-Kritisches zum Gutgläubigen Mobiliärerwerb"(1958) 23 *Rabels Zeitschrift für ausländisches und internationales Privatrecht* 1.
6. Doc. 10 § 19; Doc. 14 §§ 26-28.
7. Doc. 39 § 62 unanimous vote.
8. Doc. 18 § 37. See the detailed argument along these lines (without reference to the UNIDROIT Convention) by Bibas, S. "The Case against the Statute of Limitations" 5 *International Journal of Cultural Property* 73 at 73 at 76-77, 81-91.
9. Inglewood (Lord), "Thieves succeed where others failed" *Trace* November 1995, 4.

The principle adopted by the Study Group, though much discussed at later stages of the negotiations and at the Diplomatic Conference, achieved substantial acceptance[10].

However the protection of the *bona fide* purchaser has been seen by some to be a fundamental principle of the Civil Law encouraging the freedom of trade. Ultimately it was not thought realistic in the early nineties to expect Civil Law countries not only to reverse the rule which allowed a *bona fide* purchaser to keep the object which he had acquired but also to require him to return it without compensation for his loss[11].

Nevertheless it was a Civil Lawyer, the late Jean Chatelain, the very experienced legal counsel for the French Museums, who pointed out in a study for the European Union in 1976[12] that the existing protection of the so-called "*bona fide*" purchaser in most Civil Law systems facilitated the entry of illegally trafficked cultural objects into the licit trade.

> . . . genuinely effective protection of the property concerned is impossible without total abolition of protection for purchasers — i.e., by stipulating restitution without compensation in all cases. For speculation in art objects is such that after several successive sales they can quickly fetch considerable prices. If the legitimate owner is to be obliged to pay back the purchase price, recovery will often be impossible. Again, this would constitute indirect protection not only of the final purchaser but also of all those through whose hands the object has passed.[13]

His view was shared by another Civil Lawyer, Stefano Rodotà of Italy, in his study for the Council of Europe in 1988[14].

Professor Chatelain was not, however, the first Civil Law jurist to see the importance of changing the rules on the protection of *bona fide* purchasers where cultural objects were concerned. That was the German jurist Josef Kohler, who had already argued in 1904 that the original owner's rights should prevail, citing the case of a van Eyck painting where the owner had to pay the acquirer for its return[15].

Two other elements in the more recent discussion should be noted: the Committee of Governmental Experts which established the text of the LUAB approved the principle that

> The transferee of stolen movables cannot invoke his good faith[16].

This applied to all kinds of movables. The other is the European Convention on Offences related to Cultural Property 1985[17] which deals with criminal activity concerning cultural property. A late draft included a provision that a State could not refuse to return cultural property, even though third parties had lawfully acquired rights in the property, if the transferee had not applied the

---

10. Doc. 23 § 53; Doc. 30 § 40; Doc. 39 § 42; Doc. 48 § 48.
11. Explanatory Report 59.
12. Report cited p. 12, n. 3, 114.
13. At 144.
14. Cited p. 12, n. 4, 1.
15. Kohler, J. "Das Recht an Denkmälern und Altertumsfunden" 9 *Deutsche Juristenzeitung* (1904) 771 at 775.
16. Draft LUAB cited n.3 above, Art. 11.
17. E.T.S. No. 119. The Convention has never entered into force.

general obligation of vigilance that is incumbent upon any person who engages in transactions at large and particularly in the acquisition of rights in cultural property[18].

The UNIDROIT solution built, therefore, on a solid body of precedent scholarship and practical efforts to hinder the illicit trade in cultural property, all of which ultimately focused on some kind of change and unification of the rules concerning the *bona fide* purchaser. Without trying to make uniform rules of law on the transfer of cultural movables, an aim which would have been much more difficult of achievement, the UNIDROIT project concentrated on achieving agreement on a minimum set of uniform rules[19] which would hinder the illicit trade as far as possible, but would allow flexibility to go further in those systems which already had rules more favourable to the original owner[20]. This approach also survived through to the final text.

According to what law would a court decide whether an article was "**stolen**"? It was noted that Common Law systems do not treat conversion or fraud as theft, whereas Civil Law systems do[21]. According to the Study Group (second session), it would be the court of the State seised of the complaint to apply either its own law, or such other law as it finds applicable in accordance with its own rules of private international law[22].

The Loewe preliminary draft had restricted rights of return of stolen cultural property to material over a certain commercial value. Other suggestions were made during the course of negotiations to restrict the need to return in some way: to "outstanding objects"[23] or depending on the behaviour of the possessor[24]. But the final text maintains the rule that, without exception, every cultural object shown to have been stolen must be returned.

The word "**possessor**" is the survivor of a long debate. At least for lawyers used to working in English language systems the word "possessor", and other suggested alternatives such as "holder" and "physical possessor", had express connotations which might not be those intended by the Convention. Some would have preferred the word "owner", but, while this seems an obvious solution for systems where the *bona fide* purchaser becomes the owner, it would have created problems in those systems where the acquirer does not get title (i.e. where the *nemo dat* rule applies[25]). The word "possessor" was discussed at several sessions of experts and at the Diplomatic Conference[26], and it was finally resolved to leave it as a general, undefined, term on the understanding that its general meaning was clear and that, if its co-incidence with a particular term in a national legal system would cause problems, the implementing legislation could clarify it as appropriate.

The question of whether the person to whom the return should be made should be specified in the Convention was raised at all the sessions of Governmental Experts[27]. The third meeting of

18. De Schutter, B. "The Protection of Cultural Property: Interstate Co-operation of European Perspective" in International Institute of Higher Studies in Criminal Sciences, *The Penal Protection of Works of Art* (1983) 189.
19. See p. 20, n. 10.
20. Doc. 10 § 18.
21. Doc. 10 §§ 26-28; Doc. 14 §§ 20-22; Doc. 18, §§ 41-43; Doc. 23 §§ 54-55; Doc. 30 § 47; Doc. 39 §§ 45-47, 60; Acts 167, 168.
22. Doc. 10 § 27; Doc. 14 § 23; Doc. 18 § 45; Doc. 23 §§ 54-55; Explanatory Report § 43; Acts 167.
23. Doc. 18 § 38-39; Doc. 23 § 53; Doc. 48 §§ 29-32, Acts 161, 279.
24. Doc. 14 §§ 24-26; Doc. 18 §§ 36-39; Doc. 23 §§ 50-51; Doc. 30 § 47.
25. See p. 29 above.
26. Doc. 3 § 2; Doc. 23 §§ 50-51; Doc. 30 §§ 25, 45-46; Doc. 39 §§ 43, 59; Explanatory Report § 42, Acts 166-169, 280.
27. Doc. 3 Art. 2 "to the dispossessed person"; Doc. 23 § 52; Doc. 30, 10; Doc. 39 § 44; Doc. 48 § 71.

Governmental Experts adopted the view of the Study Group; that the object would be returned to the dispossessed person and that it would be for the court, which was accustomed to deciding questions of ownership and conflicts of legal interests, to decide who that person should be: it could be a museum where the item was on loan, or creditor with whom the object had been deposited[28].

Article 3(2)

> For the purposes of this Convention, a cultural object which has been unlawfully excavated or lawfully excavated but unlawfully retained shall be considered stolen, when consistent with the law of the State where the excavation took place.

The vexed question of how to handle clandestinely excavated cultural objects is illustrated clearly by the history of Article 3(2). In the United States there has been a long debate on the subject, some asserting that an object should not be regarded as stolen unless it has previously been "reduced into the possession" of the claimant[29]. This view has not been accepted by courts in the United States[30] and, as has been pointed out, declarations of State ownership of subsoil resources, whether oil, minerals or archaeological resources, have long been accepted as constructive ownership in the Common Law and therefore a wrongful taking must be considered as theft[31]. Many States have laws vesting undiscovered antiquities in the State, others in the landowner[32]. Where title is vested in the State, why should the claimant State not be able to sue for theft?

Behind this theoretical issue lies the problem of proof of identity of an illegally excavated cultural object which is unlikely to have been seen by the landowner or by the State before it is offered for sale on a foreign market. Occasional cases have arisen where proof of identity has been made out, although sometimes by the most painstaking methods. In one case previously buried wooden sculptures were satisfactorily identified because of a pre-existing photograph showing a spade cut which had occurred when the digger had located them[33]. In another case an illegally excavated idol was sufficiently identified by the chemical composition of the bronze, stylistic elements, and the pattern of termite tracks over the surface, all three elements shared by another eleven idols of the same suite known to have been excavated at the same time and still in India[34].

---

28. Doc. 18 § 46; Doc. 39 §§ 44, 59, Lalive, P. "La Convention d'UNIDROIT sur les biens culturels ou illicitement exportés (du 24 juin 1995)" 1997 *Revue suisse de Droit international et de Droit européen* 13, 33.

29. A similar view was put forward in the Study Group but rejected, Doc. 18 §§ 149-156.

30. *United States v. McClain* 545 F.2d 988 (1977); 551 F.2d 52 (1977); 593 F.2d 658 (1979) [U.S.].

31. Gerstenblith, P. Contribution to "The Cultural Property Round Table" organized by the Committee on Art Law of the New York Bar Association, 12 November 1996, 3-4; *U.S. v. Gerber* 999 F.2d 1112 (7th cir. 1993); Palmer, N. "Treasure Trove and Title to Discovered Antiquities" 2 *International Journal of Cultural Property* (1993) 275 at 277. "Objects which satisfy the legal definition of treasure trove are the property of the Crown or its franchisee. To remove treasure trove with the intention of permanently depriving the Crown or its franchisee of it constitutes the crime of theft . . ."

32. The UNESCO Recommendation on the International Principles Applicable to Archaeological Excavations 1956 recommends that States define the status of the archaeological sub-soil and, where State ownership of the said sub-soil is recognised, specifically mention the fact in its legislation (Principle 5(e)).

33. The identification was no longer disputed at the time of hearing: *Attorney-General of New Zealand v. Ortiz* [1982] 2 W.L.R. 10; [1982] 3 W.L.R. 570; [1983] 2 W.L.R. 809; [1984] A.C. 1 (H.L.) [United Kingdom].

34. *Bumper Development Corp. Ltd. v. Comr. of Police* [1991] 4 All E.R. 638 [United Kingdom].

The special problems of clandestine excavation had already been considered in the study group[35] which foresaw products of such illegal activity as coming under Chapter II where they could be proved to have been stolen and under Chapter III in other cases. At the first meeting of Governmental Experts, Mexico proposed that all illegally excavated objects be considered as stolen[36]. This was rejected at the second meeting of Governmental Experts[37]. At the third meeting the United States Delegation proposed an article (now Article 3(2)) of similar content to the Mexican proposal[38] and it was adopted by 42 votes to none with five abstentions. It not only survived discussion at the fourth meeting of Governmental Experts[39], but an additional clause was added to Article 5 allowing a request for the return of a cultural object taken from a site contrary to the law applicable to the excavation of cultural objects and removed from that State[40]! At the Diplomatic Conference Japan (which had not been represented at the meetings of experts) and the United States proposed the deletion of Article 3(2)[41]. This surprising turn of events did not, however, draw the sympathy of the majority of delegates, and the article was maintained[42].

Why the change of view? The United States negotiators on the text of the UNESCO Convention 1970 had insisted on the insertion of Articles 7 and 9 of that Convention which restricted (in their view) the application of the provisions on theft to "cultural property stolen from a museum or a religious or secular public monument or similar institution in another State party . . . provided that such property is documented as appertaining to the inventory of that institution" while the provisions on illegally excavated goods were limited to countries which had additional bilateral agreements with the United States[43] or emergency conditions "of crisis proportions"[44]. This meant that claimants for illegally excavated objects either had to negotiate a special agreement with the United States or bring a lawsuit themselves under the Common law rules on theft, rather than have the United States government act for them in accordance with the Convention.

However there seemed to be some confusion in the 1990s about the position of the United States' own cultural heritage: an increasing concern for the loss of indigenous Native American material gave an incentive to try to ensure that clandestinely excavated cultural objects could be recovered from other countries and, as the provisions of the UNIDROIT text on theft apply to all cultural objects as opposed to the limited categories covered by the provisions on export, there was an incentive to include them in Chapter II rather than Chapter III. This seems to have been compounded by a misunderstanding: the statutory prohibition of export of such objects from the United States is included in the "Archaeological Resources Protection Act"[45] which, it may have been considered, would, on some of the proposals of Article 1(b) in the narrowest formulations, not have been included. At any rate, it seems clear that the present formulation "law regulating the export of cultural objects for the purpose of protecting its cultural heritage" would certainly include that legislation, the purpose of which is to protect archaeological resources and which makes it illegal to move across national or international boundaries property which has been the subject of an

---

35. Doc. 14 §§ 32, 53.
36. Doc. 23 § 56, 164-165.
37. Doc. 30 §§ 22-25, 47, 104-106.
38. Doc. 38, Misc 14; Doc. 39 §§ 36-37, 47, 63.
39. Doc. 48 §§ 49-50.
40. Doc. 48 §§ 49-50; 109-115.
41. Acts 169.
42. Acts 169-172, 281-282.
43. The United States *Convention on Cultural Property Implementation Act* 1983, 19 U.S.C. s.2601 requires the signature of such an agreement before the United States will impose an import ban (s. 303).
44. Id. s. 304.
45. 16 U.S.C. §§ 470aa *et seq.*

offence against State or Federal law (such as illicit excavation or theft). Be that as it may, the confused history of this provision shows that the issue is a difficult one.

The result of the inclusion of Article 3(2) as well as of 5(3)(a), (b) and (c) and the final phrase of Article 5(3) means that most clandestinely excavated objects will be able to be sued for either under Article 3(2) (if proof of identity can be established) or under Article 5(3) (by proof that the object was subject to export control and that no export permit was granted). Whereas an owner can sue under Article 3, a State sues under Article 5: where that State is also the owner it therefore has the option to proceed either under Article 3 or under Article 5.

It should be noted that "**excavation**" applies to underwater sites in accordance with the usual interpretation applied in national legislation[46] and the express provisions of the 1956 UNESCO Recommendation on the International Principles Applicable to Archaeological Excavations (§ 1).

Article 3 Sections 3, 4, 5, 6, 7 and 8

Of all the issues debated in the preparation of the text, that of limitation was probably the most difficult. Dr. Loewe's preliminary draft had proposed a general limitation of 30 years for objects of high commercial value and 10 years for those of more limited value[47]. A redraft of the section embodied the current form of an absolute limit running from the date of theft and a much shorter one running from the date of the despoiled owner's knowledge or imputed knowledge of the whereabouts of the object[48]. This came to be discussed in detail at the third session of the Study Group[49]. As the UNIDROIT Secretariat reported, while some members of the group preferred a short period so as to respect the requirements of the art market, others preferred a relatively long period which would take account of the speculative aspect (purchase of the cultural object as an investment[50]). Others went so far as to suggest that there should be no limitation period for cultural objects of very great importance or for archives[51] or for claims brought by a State[52] (bearing in mind that in some countries, such as France, almost all museum holdings are State property). Yet others wanted to have no limitation period whatever[53]. It was necessary to explain the important functions of limitation periods in those countries which used them[54].

The bifold solution chosen which survived, after much discussion, through to the Diplomatic Conference, has much to commend it. It reflects rules in several legal systems such as the longer rules for limitation relating to State property or even inalienability; or general longer terms of limitation such as 30 years, as well as relative periods of limitation based on knowledge of the claimant.

There was vigorous debate on limitations provisions at the meetings of Governmental Experts[55]. At the third meeting in 1993 it was decided to leave alternatives in brackets for the length of the periods which would have to be resolved at the Diplomatic Conference[56].

---

46. Doc. 48 § 137.
47. Doc. 3, Art. 2(4); Doc. 10 § 53; Doc. 14 § 64.
48. Doc. 18 §§ 49-51 discussed Doc. 23 §§ 57-60; Doc. 30 §§ 48-54, 57-58.
49. Doc. 39 §§ 48-52, 56-62.
50. See, as to this aspect, the comments of Bibas, in the article mentioned n. 8, above.
51. Acts 180 (Mariani).
52. Doc. 18 §§ 57-61.
53. Doc. 48 § 62; Acts 178 (Foroutan).
54. Doc. 30 § 49; Acts 179 (Fraoua).
55. Doc. 23, §§ 57-61; Doc. 30 §§ 48-54; Doc. 39 §§ 48-62; Doc. 48 §§ 51, 73.
56. Doc. 48 § 55.

There the voting on these provisions, as on others, favoured the views of "exporting" States i.e. with long periods of limitation. This upset the delicate balance wrought at the fourth meeting of Governmental Experts where "importing" States had accepted a longer absolute period of limitation (50 years, with special rules for certain categories of material) provided that there was a very short one based on knowledge by the claimant of either the location of the object or the identity of the holder.

The issue of limitation became one of the key issues to be settled by the special working group which produced the compromise text and the present wording of these sections is the work of that compromise group. While the substance could have been expressed much more economically and elegantly, it was in fact hammered out in such a way as to include key phrases which would make it acceptable to national governments. The complicated text was the price of general acceptance at the conference.

Article 3(3)

> Any claim for restitution shall be brought within a period of three years from the time when the claimant knew the location of the cultural object and the identity of its possessor, and in any case within a period of fifty years from the time of the theft.

The use of the phrase "**from the time when the claimant knew the location of the cultural object and the identity of its possessor**" is based on a provision inserted during the third meeting of the Study Group[57]. It is more generous to the robbed owner than those systems which measure the beginning of the time limit for claims from the date of the theft or loss (France[58]), or from the date on which the possessor in good faith acquired the object (England[59]); is similar to those systems which use the date of discovery of the object[60] (New Jersey, California) but less generous than those which use the date of demand and refusal[61] (New York courts). The practice of the latter courts has enabled claims to be made for the recovery of important cultural objects 21[62], and 36[63] years after the date of the theft. The use of a more generous period for the owner to act seems a fair way to resolve issues of missing cultural property where the owner has been diligent but, because of the international and covert nature of many transactions, has no way of asserting his claim because he cannot trace the property.

---

57. Doc. 18 §§ 50-51.
58. *Civil Code* Art. 2279.
59. See n. 2 above.
60. *O'Keeffe v. Snyder* 405 A.2d 840 (1979) at first instance, reviewed 416 A. 2d 862 where the Supreme Court of New Jersey decided that the cause of action accrued and hence the date from which the limitation should be measured was "when she first knew, or reasonably should have known through the exercise of due diligence" of the cause of action; *The Regents of the University of California v. Salvato et al.* Action No. 1 BC 114151 Superior Court of Los Angeles discussed in Shapreau, C. "California's Discovery Rule is Applied to Delay Accrual of Replevin Claims in Cases Involving Stolen Art" 1 *Art Antiquity and Law* (1996) 407.
61. *Menzel v. List* 253 N.Y.S. 2d 43 Misc. 2d 300; 267 N.Y.S.2d 804 aff'd 298 N.Y.S. 2d 979 (1969); *Kunstsammlung zu Weimar v. Elicofon* 536 F. Supp. 829 (1981) 678 F. 2d 1150 (1982); *Solomon R. Guggenheim Foundation v. Lubell* 567 N.Y.S.2d 623 (1991).
62. *Menzel v. List* , *Kunstsammlungen zu Weimar v. Elicofon*, both cited last note; both claims made after more than 20 years.
63. *De Weerth v. Baldinger* 836 F.2d. 1150 (1987).

The recent discovery of large amounts of cultural property taken in the course of or in the immediate aftermath of World War II[64] shows that long limitation periods have important reasons behind them, and it is noteworthy that the neither the Declaration of London of 1943 concerning the restitution of cultural property taken under Nazi occupation[65] nor the Protocol to the Convention on the Protection of Cultural Property in the Event of Armed Conflict 1954 (the "Hague Convention"), which concerns displaced cultural movables, has an expressed limitation period. An expert on the Declaration specifically stated that it had no limitation period and that

> For the first time in history, restitution may be expected to continue for as long as works of art known to have been plundered during a war continue to be rediscovered[66].

Norway proposed a 20 year limitation period for the 1954 Protocol, but since this was defeated, Toman concludes that

> there is no time-limit for lodging a claim for the return of property[67].

Cultural objects taken during conflict or occupation would fall within the ambit of the Convention in any event[68]. The Israeli Delegation sought to have a clause inserted stating that the running of the limitation period would be interrupted if it were not possible to bring a claim, such as the case where the two countries concerned were at war[69]. Although this proposal was not accepted, the rules concerning interruptions to the running of limitation periods would in any case apply to claims under the Convention. However, it should be noted that if the limitation periods have expired under the UNIDROIT Convention, a remedy may still be available under the 1954 Protocol[70].

As a compromise between those favouring the shortest possible periods and those unhappy with any limitations at all, the provision for extended periods for certain categories of material was proposed[71] which is now to be found in Article 3(5) and 3(7).

The text which emerged from the Study Group of Experts contained different periods of limitation for stolen (three and thirty years) and for illegally exported cultural objects(five and twenty years)[72]. Since some objects are both stolen and illegally exported, it was important that these periods should be the same: this was finally achieved at the third session of Governmental Experts[73]. In

---

64. In 1990 the case of the Quedlinburg treasures was revealed: these very important cultural objects (early Gospels, reliquaries etc.) were stolen from the treasury of a Convent Church at the end of World War II by a United States soldier and were being sold by his successors in 1990 - 45 years after the theft. The conference on *Spoils of War* held in New York from 19-21 January 1995 showed that, in addition to many art treasures only recently revealed, such as that of the so-called "Priam's treasure" from Troy, formerly in Berlin, there were still many other discoveries being made. Proceedings published as *The Spoils of War* (New York, 1997) ed. By Simpson, E.
65. For the text of this declaration and a discussion of its contents and application see book cited p. 24, n. 23, 805-811.
66. Hall, A.R. "The Recovery of Cultural Objects Dispersed During World War II" 1951 *Department of State Bulletin* [United States] 339. See the similar comment of Hosain (Pakistan), also mentioning that the UNESCO Convention 1970 has no express limitation period, Acts 173.
67. Toman, J. *The Protection of Cultural Property in the Event of Armed Conflict* (Aldershot U.K. and Paris) 1996, 345; published in French as *La Protection de Biens culturels en cas de Conflit armé* (UNESCO, Paris) 1994.
68. P. 24, n. 27 (Croatia) and related text.
69. Doc. 30 § 149; Doc. 39 § 149.
70. There are currently 88 States party to the Convention and 75 to the Protocol. They are listed in Appendix V.
71. Doc. 23 §§ 57-61, Doc. 30 §§ 48-51; Doc. 39 §§ 49-50, 56-57.
72. Doc. 18, Annex III, Arts. 3(2), 7(b).
73. Doc. 40, Preliminary draft convention on stolen or illegally exported cultural objects, Arts. 3(3), 7(2).

addition, States favouring shorter limitation periods accepted a longer absolute period (50 years instead of 30) on condition that the shorter relative period (three years instead of one) was adopted[74]. Though some argued for one year (which is the limitation period in the European Directive of 15 March 1993 on the return of cultural objects unlawfully removed from the territory of a Member State, Appendix XI) this was felt to be impractical when applied to a convention of universal, rather than regional, application[75].

Another point of discussion was whether the knowledge of the location or the identity of the possessor should be sufficient for the shorter limitation period to start running, or whether the plaintiff should know both before the period started running[76]. The final text makes knowledge of both elements necessary before time would begin to run. Droz has pointed out that it would be dangerous to start the time limit running when the robbed owner knows only the identity of the possessor, since he or she could only too easily, once alerted by a request for restitution, place the object in a bank vault in a non-Contracting State[77].

The language "or ought reasonably to have known" was part of the original formulation. It was much discussed and finally omitted at the Diplomatic Conference[78]. Some developing States seemed to feel that these words could be used to block their claims; others felt that such words were well understood in many legal systems; that judges are able to justly assess what is reasonable in such circumstances. However, as knowledge is in the mind of the claimant, it would seem difficult for a court ever to have absolute evidence in this respect, and as one delegate to the fourth meeting of Governmental Experts put it

> it was probable that judges in many States would in any event apply the general rules of their law in respect of an unreasonable delay on the part of a claimant in discovering the identity of the possessor or the location of the object[79].

An interesting parallel can be made to the discussion of similar words in reference to Articles 4(1) and 6(1) concerning the knowledge or constructive knowledge of theft or illicit export on the part of an acquirer who is required to return the object concerned, where these words were retained.

If such knowledge can be imputed, what sort of evidence would courts be likely to choose? One reason why States with major problems of illicit export and theft were wary of these phrases could have been that they were alarmed by suggestions which have at times been made that appearance in an auction or exhibition catalogue in another country might be sufficient to impute knowledge to a claimant. However it should be noted that courts in systems which apply such tests have been reasonable in finding that knowledge must have been not only accessible, but reasonably likely to have reached the claimant[80] and that a bill presented a few years ago to the New York legislature which would have made museum exhibition of a piece sufficient to base the starting of the New York limitation period was defeated[81]. On the other hand, an acquirer who has made real and appropriate efforts to notify possible owners of the transfer at the time of

---

74. Acts 172-176.
75. Acts 173 (Australia), 174 (Japan), 176 (UNESCO).
76. Doc. 23 §§ 62-64; Doc. 30 §§ 53-54, 59; Doc. 39, §§ 53-55, 65; Doc. 48 §§ 56-61; Acts 172-176.
77. Droz, art. cited p. 22, n. 4 § 20.
78. Doc. 23 §§ 62-64; Doc. 30 §§ 53-54, 59; Doc. 39, §§ 53-55; Doc. 48 §§ 56-61; Acts 172-176.
79. Doc. 48 § 56.
80. For a full discussion of points at which the limitation period has been held to start running, such as the date of theft, the date of discovery, the date of demand and refusal, see book cited p. 24, n. 23, 416-428.
81. Id., 426-428; Nafziger, J. "Repose Legislation: a Threat to the Protection of the World's Cultural Heritage" 17 *California Western International Law Journal* (1987) 250.

his prospective acquisition should expect that the shorter limitation period will apply. This may include notification of a government from whose territory the object is likely to have come. Mere inclusion in a public collection, temporary exhibition or auction catalogue would not be sufficient.

Article 3(4)

> However, a claim for restitution of a cultural object forming an integral part of an identified monument or archaeological site, or belonging to a public collection, shall not be subject to time limitations other than a period of three years from the time when the claimant knew the location of the cultural object and the identity of its possessor.

This provision follows a proposal, introduced at the third session of Governmental Experts, that there should be no limitation period for certain very important cultural objects[82]. Such a proposal would have satisfied those countries which provided for the inalienability and imprescriptibility of certain cultural property such as that owned by the State[83]. However certain experts were vigorously opposed to having no limitations period at all for any category of cultural objects[84]. At the fourth meeting of experts Greece was anxious to introduce a provision that country had succeeded in achieving at the negotiations for the European Directive, for a prescriptive limit to be extended to 75 years for inventoried objects from "public collections" or "ecclesiastical collections"[85]. The latter terminology was not, of course, appropriate to an international, as opposed to a regional, convention, since it was narrowly directed at a particularly European phenomenon. How to define the special class of objects to which some lengthened period of claim should be given became the subject of an extended debate and was only ultimately resolved by the special working group which produced the compromise text.

It was only at the Diplomatic Conference that, again on the proposal of the Greek delegation, the words "**monument, archaeological site**" were inserted. These words do, however, somewhat reflect the wording of Article 7 of the 1970 UNESCO Convention, which speak of "cultural property stolen from . . . a religious or secular monument".

Article 3(5)

> Notwithstanding the provisions of the preceding paragraph, any Contracting State may declare that a claim is subject to a time limitation of 75 years or such longer period as is provided in its law. A claim made in another Contracting State for restitution of a cultural object displaced from a monument, archaeological site or public collection in a Contracting State making such a declaration shall also be subject to that time limitation.

At the Diplomatic Conference the Committee of the Whole voted for the recognition by all Contracting States of the inalienability of an object from a monument, archaeological site or public collection[86]. This was quite unacceptable to certain States (in particular, the Netherlands

---

82. Doc. 39 §§ 57-58, §§ 66-67; Doc. 48 §§ 62, 69.
83. Doc. 39 § 56; Doc. 48, § 63; Acts 283.
84. Doc. 48 § 69; Acts 174 (Mexico).
85. European Council Directive 93/7/EEC 15 March 1993 (text given in Appendix XI), Arts. 1 & 7; Doc. 39 §§ 57-58, 66-67; Doc. 48 §§ 63-70, 74-79; Acts 177-181, 283-285.
86. Acts 283-285.

and Switzerland, which were active members of the working group, and the United Kingdom, which was not). They insisted that inalienability would render the Convention impossible to accept in their countries[87]. The working group therefore developed this provision allowing a State to establish an absolute limit of 75 years to claims for public collections, although it was, for political reasons, expressed as an exception to the general rule in Article 3(4). Nonetheless its substance was crucial in the negotiations.

Article 3(6)

> A declaration referred to in the preceding paragraph shall be made at the time of signature, ratification, acceptance, approval or accession.

It is clear that States who hold strongly to the importance of limitation periods will all make the declaration suggested. If they do not, only the three year period from knowledge of location and identity of the possessor will apply, and claims can continue to be made *ad infinitum*. The effect is likely to be, therefore, that States with strong art markets will adopt the 75 year period as the maximum in which a claim can be brought under the Convention, and States which presently provide for imprescriptibility of some classes of cultural property will continue to apply that rule. They will not, however, be bound to extend this longer period to claims under the Convention from States which do not provide a longer period for claims made in their own jurisdictions.

It is important to note that all these limitation provisions will only apply to claims under the UNIDROIT Convention. The Convention is not retroactive (Article 10). They do not provide any cutoff for other claims, such as those arising out of displacements during and immediately after World War II or in colonial times, which can still be pursued by other means, such as bilateral negotiations or through the UNESCO Intergovernmental Committee for Promoting the Return of Cultural Property to its Countries of Origin or its Restitution in Case of Illicit Appropriation.

Article 3(7)

> For the purposes of this Convention, a "public collection" consists of a group of inventoried or otherwise identified cultural objects owned by:
>
> (a) a Contracting State
>
> (b) a regional or local authority of a Contracting State;
>
> (c) a religious institution in a Contracting State; or
>
> (d) an institution that is established for an essentially cultural, educational or scientific purpose in a Contracting State and is recognized in that State as serving the public interest.

Considerable work had gone on at the fourth meeting of Governmental Experts[88] to define "**public collection**" and this work has been reflected in the final text of this provision. The concern, particularly of the United States delegation, was to have a provision which would include material

---

87. Acts 283-284 (Sweden, Switzerland, United Kingdom, United States).
88. Doc. 48, §§ 63-68, 77-79.

from its museum collections, almost all of which would not necessarily fall within the description "public collections". The concern of many other States was to limit this exception as far as possible so that the stricter rules of limitation were the norm, rather than the exception.

Article 3(8)

In addition, a claim for restitution of a sacred or communally important cultural object belonging to and used by a tribal or indigenous community in a Contracting State as part of that community's traditional or ritual use, shall be subject to the time limitation applicable to public collections.

It was at the fourth meeting of experts that the Australian delegation, strongly supported by the Canadian delegation, pointed out that "public collections" necessarily excluded many objects of supreme importance in use in traditional communities and that the implications of this were significant[89]. While most communities would survive the loss of a public collection, many traditional communities are devastated to the point of the destruction of their traditional culture by the loss from the community of sacred or secret objects. Many delegations were not familiar with these problems and there was not sufficient time at the fourth session to adequately discuss the proposal.

UNESCO, in its comments for the Diplomatic Conference[90], pointed out that it could not support a text which in effect discriminated against these traditional communities (especially in the year beginning the Decade of Indigenous Peoples!). The Australian and Canadian Delegations introduced a new proposal at the Diplomatic Conference which spoke of

> ... a claim for restitution of a sacred and secret object belonging to and used by a member or members of an indigenous community in a Contracting State as part of that community's cultural practice ...[91]

This was reformulated and proposed as a compromise provision by the United States, with the support of Australia and Canada, in the form in which it at present appears[92].

The phrase "**indigenous**" can be interpreted by reference to the considerable documentation which has developed within United Nations practice (Appendices VI and VII). "**Tribal**" includes groups which may not come within that categorization (perhaps are majority peoples in their State) but are tribally organized.

---

89. Doc. 48, § 76.
90. Acts 96-97.
91. Acts 122.
92. See discussion Acts 177-178, 180, 265-266, 285-286.

ARTICLE 4

It will be recalled that Chatelain[1] thought that no compensation should be given to a person returning a cultural object to the owner from whom it had been stolen. This view had many adherents in all stages of the negotiation of the text[2]. However some experts pointed out that requiring return from a *bona fide* purchaser was already a very considerable change in a fundamental principle of law for a number of legal systems, and that to do so without compensation would be extremely difficult for political reasons[3]. The compromise was therefore to make provision for compensation, but only for acquirers who could prove their diligence. The principle of compensation also served another role: the prospect of losing compensation otherwise available would encourage potential acquirers to refrain from purchasing such objects in the absence of adequate information, which would discourage theft, and, at the same time, alter the present practice of dealers and auction houses of not disclosing the names of sellers, and that of purchasers of not questioning the statements of sellers[4]. (Note, however, that compensation will only be available in those States not applying rules more favourable to return to the despoiled owner — see Article 9 below).

Dr. Loewe's preliminary draft made no mention of the words *bona fide* or "good faith". This wise approach avoided problems of definition (because definitions of good faith vary considerably between systems) and also avoided the possibility of judges consciously or unconsciously importing into their application of the Convention national doctrines already long developed on this terminology. Instead, the UNIDROIT Convention uses the concept of "due diligence" and provides a list of some of the elements which a judge is to use in his assessment of whether this test has been met. This is not an exclusive list, and other elements have been mentioned. These have included the provisions of the contract, the circumstances in which it was concluded, the provenance of the object, any special circumstances in respect of the transferor's acquisition of the object which are known to the possessor, any reasonably accessible information as to whether the cultural object had been exported legally[5].

Article 4(1)

> The possessor of a stolen cultural object required to return it shall be entitled, at the time of its restitution, to payment of fair and reasonable compensation provided that the possessor neither knew nor ought reasonably to have known that the object was stolen and can prove that it exercised due diligence when acquiring the object.

The phrase "**fair and reasonable compensation**" was, as may be expected, the result of much discussion which was not resolved more easily at UNIDROIT than it has been at any other international negotiations over the last 30 years. Dr. Loewe's preliminary draft spoke of "the

---

1. Quoted above, p. 30, n. 13.
2. Doc. 10 § 29; Doc. 23 § 68; Doc. 30 §§ 60-74; Doc. 39, §§ 68-71; Doc. 48 §§ 82-83; Acts 184 (Izadi), 185 (Zimba Chabala), 187 (Ghofrani).
3. Doc. 23 §§ 69-71, 73.
4. Doc. 48 § 81.
5. Acts 98.

price paid . . or a sum corresponding to the actual value of the property at the place where it is located"[6]. At the second meeting of the Study Group a proposal was made for "an equitable sum which should exceed neither the price paid nor the actual value"[7]. Others wished to speak of "equitable compensation". Both these formulae would leave a discretion to the judge to take account of the relevant factors as between the claimant and the returning party. A compromise phrase "equitable compensation having regard to the situation of the two parties" was settled on[8]. At the following meeting of the Study group "fair and reasonable compensation" was chosen for the English version of the text over the word "equitable" which, it was pointed out, might cause misunderstanding in legal systems where it already had a clearly defined legal meaning[9]. At the third meeting discussion centred around the desirability or not of having the commercial value set as a maximum: some thought that expressing that in the text might encourage the judge to give it extra weight in deciding what was fair and reasonable, and one expert pointed out that "fair and reasonable" was a universal concept with a strict limit, and another that it had been applied in the context of nationalisation for a long time and that the sum was often less, and sometimes very much less, than the actual commercial value[10]. It was felt important to accord the judge a certain amount of flexibility for it may be necessary to take into account money which could be due to the holder under a warranty from a seller to him or her: clearly the holder should not be entitled to recover twice for the returned object. Professor Norman Palmer has recently pointed out that if the UNIDROIT Convention is implemented in any country, the implied warranty for quiet possession of an art object sold by a professional in England will imply a liability of the seller for claims which result in the return of the item, whether for theft or illegal export[11].

Some delegates thought that the measure "fair and reasonable compensation" placed too heavy a load on developing countries[12]. At the second meeting of the Study Group, mention had already been made of the possibility of establishing a Fund for countries (in this case owners, or countries subventioning citizens who were owners) who would find the costs of compensation and litigation far beyond their resources[13].

The possibility of such a Fund was discussed in detail at the first three meetings of the UNESCO Intergovernmental Committee for Promoting the Return of Cultural Property to Its Countries of Origin or Its Restitution in Case of Illicit Appropriation (1981-1985), but no agreement was reached. There are certain problems with such a Fund: what should it cover? Insurance, transport and re-installation costs are relatively uncontroversial, but are usually not so large that they cannot be covered by *ad hoc* arrangements e.g. by a private donor. Legal fees are another matter — in some countries these are so astronomical that some ceiling would have to be placed on the amount to be made available. It is also questionable whether wealthy States would donate to a Fund which would basically go into the pockets of its own lawyers to deprive some of their own citizens of cultural property currently held by them, in order to benefit another country — in general more direct support for another country's culture is the preferred kind of aid. Finally there is the question of compensation: and this is the most difficult of all, because if purchasers are sure of getting compensation, they will obviously fight harder to prove their diligence and courts may tend to be more gentle with them than when faced by an indigent plaintiff. It is a fact

---

6. Doc. 3, Art. 3(1).
7. Doc. 14 § 41.
8. Doc. 14 §§ 42-43.
9. Doc. 18 § 54, 61-62.
10. Doc. 18 § 62. See the discussion on this point in Lalive, art. cited p. 32, n. 28, 36-37.
11. Statement to the Conference "Law and Art: the Free Movement of Cultural Property" Maastricht 6-7 March 1997.
12. Doc. 23 § 67.
13. Doc. 14 § 44; Doc. 23 §§ 68-71.

that in many cases the dispossessed owner will either be the State (e.g. the object comes from the State museums or is a subsoil find vested in the State), or will be entirely supported by the State because the owner is not itself in a position to sue (e.g. an indigenous community[14] or an impoverished temple[15]).

Nonetheless the possibility of such a Fund being established was an important factor in persuading developing States to accept the duty to compensate even for the limited group of diligent purchasers, and a proposal for such a Fund, made by the Italian Delegation at the Eighth session of the UNESCO Intergovernmental Committee was reiterated at the UNIDROIT Conference by the Italian delegation. It is currently under consideration at UNESCO.

It is to be noted that Article 4 makes no provision for the costs of restitution, although this is regulated in respect of the costs of return of illicitly exported objects (Article 6(4)). The matter was discussed, but it was felt that this was one of the elements which could be taken into account by the judge in assessing "fair and reasonable compensation"[16].

Another element considered was the possible reimbursement of restoration costs[17]. This was also not included, neither here, nor in respect of illegally exported cultural objects (see discussion on Article 6). Under Japanese law the possessor of an object belonging to another person is — if he has to return it — entitled to compensation for the amount of the costs of maintenance and conservation of the object, irrespective of whether or not he knew or ought to have known that the object was stolen, and the Japanese Delegate argued for this view at the Diplomatic Conference[18].

In the case of *Webb v. A.-G. for Ireland*[19] a judge of the Irish High Court, while awarding title to the finders of a ninth century hoard which had been deposited with the national museum, took into account the cost of conservation by the Museum which had substantially increased the value of the object. (The Supreme Court on appeal, however, awarded title to the Irish State). However where cultural objects are in the hands of private persons it is important not to encourage a possessor to undertake activities which might in fact not be in the interests of the heritage: the dealer holding a well documented Northern Kwakiutl Thunderbird headdress which was refused export permission in Canada used the period before the appeal for extensive "restoration" work. The action had the effect, which was for him convenient, of very substantially increasing the price (offered by a United States client) while at the same time raising questions about the integrity of the object as so "restored". At any rate no Canadian museum was prepared to pay the asking price[20]. The Archaeological Institute of America, in its comments on the preliminary draft Convention, said

> ... no compensation should be paid for any restoration or conservation work on a cultural object. Members of the committee had consulted professional conservators who also shared this belief and pointed out that in some instances compensation might have to be paid for restoration work of poor quality, on work that actually detracted from or damaged the integrity

---

14. Such as the Maori tribe the Taranaki involved in the *Ortiz* case cited p. 32, n. 33 above.
15. Such as the ruined Hindu temple, which nonetheless had retained its juristic personality in Hindu law, which was a plaintiff in the *Bumper Development* case cited above p. 32, n. 34.
16. Doc. 39 §§ 72, 170; Acts 187 (Shimizu), 188 (UNESCO).
17. Doc. 30 §§ 60, 73.
18. Shimizu, Acts 187.
19. [1988] 8 *ILRM* (Irish Law Reports Monthly) 565.
20. This case is discussed in detail in book cited p. 24, n. 23, 544.

of the object, while in other cases the possessor of a cultural object that is to be returned might engage in restoration work in the hope of receiving additional payment from the country of origin[21].

Apparently the Diplomatic Conference accepted the possible unwisdom of automatically providing reimbursement for conservation[22] for it did not adopt it. It is evident, however, that a judge might take this factor into account in assessing fair and reasonable compensation where the object was conserved by a reputable institution, as was the case in *Webb v. Ireland*, if in fact he is convinced that there was no ulterior motive in the action taken and that the conservation measures have not caused the deterioration or loss in cultural or commercial value of the object and especially if lack of proper conservation would have led to a natural deterioration endangering the survival of the object.

The wording "**neither knew nor ought reasonably to have known**" which now appears in Articles 4(1) and 6(1), both referring to an acquirer, was originally matched by equivalent wording in Articles 3(4) and 5(5) referring to knowledge by the dispossessed owner of the whereabouts of the object and the identity of the possessor. The omission of the wording in Articles 3(4) and 5(5) raises the question of whether a judge should now interpret this to mean a difference in the test for knowledge of an acquirer to that required of a dispossessed owner. It was pointed out that this appears to be a lack of consistency in the text and that it might be thought unfair or discriminatory. The majority was unconvinced by the argument and the differential wording was adopted[23]. However, the judge will still have to be satisfied that the claimant did not know: a mere assertion on his part, when all the evidence points the other way, will not be sufficient.

It should be noted that serious collectors already undertake various inquiries when buying important cultural property: expert opinions, for example, as to the authenticity and condition of a piece. These inquiries frequently become historical inquiries (for example, to eliminate the possibility that the piece is a copy often requires research into the history of the item's previous sale and possession). A due inquiry into provenance is, therefore, no unreasonable additional requirement to satisfy, viewed against the range of precautions that a buyer should normally take.

The notion "**at the time of its restitution**" has been in the text since the Loewe preliminary draft. It does not seem to have been discussed. It would seem to ensure that compensation is paid immediately on the return, and not by way of scheduled payments or in a blocked currency not immediately available to the person returning the object. Payment arrangements, however, if not settled by the decision of the court or other competent authority, may be negotiated. The return of a stolen Siva Nataraja to India was postponed to enable the acquirer, a United States collector, to display it for ten years[24]. Such an arrangement may enable an owner which has difficulty raising the compensation immediately to ensure the return of the item even if delayed. It may also be a solution for an owner who finds a difficulty of principle in paying over money for what it regards as its own property.

---

21. Professional Responsibilities Committee, Subcommittee on the Unidroit Convention, "Comments on the Preliminary Draft Unidroit Convention on Stolen or Illegally Exported cultural Objects" 22 September 1993.
22. Acts 188.
23. Acts 299-300.
24. *Union of India v. The Norton Simon Foundation* United States District Court, Southern District of New York, 74 Cir. 5331; United States District Court, Central District of California, Case No. CV 74-3581-RJK. The case and the settlement were discussed in DuBoff, L.D. *The Deskbook of Art Law*, 1977. 109-14; Sayre, C.F. "Cultural Property Laws in India and Japan" 33 *UCLA Law Review* 1986, 876-79.

Article 4(2)

> Without prejudice to the right of the possessor to compensation referred to in the preceding paragraph, reasonable efforts shall be made to have the person who transferred the cultural object to the possessor, or any prior transferor, pay the compensation where to do so would be consistent with the law of the State in which the claim is brought.

The question was raised as to who should pay the compensation[25]. At the third meeting of Governmental Experts a proposal, first made at the second session, was revived, which would permit a third party to guarantee payment of the compensation in place of an owner who would be financially incapable of so doing. The Committee voted against its adoption on the ground that it was of no practical utility, if only because it had no normative substance. (A similar proposal was made regarding the payment by another person of compensation in relation to illegally exported cultural objects, but it was defeated[26].)

On the other hand there was a consensus that the Convention did not require the owner itself to pay compensation and that it was not intended to exclude a system of sponsorship or other method of paying compensation[27].

At the fourth meeting of Governmental Experts it had been proposed that compensation could only be claimed from a person to whom return is ordered if it had "exhausted all the remedies of compensation against the transferor of the object"[28]. The proposal was not voted on. As a thief can usually not be found, and many transferors in a series of transactions would create a difficult set of litigations, this proposal did not meet with favour, although it was appreciated that the aim was to help claimants who had difficulties in paying the compensation.

The concern behind these proposals entered discussion again at the Diplomatic Conference. A reference was made to the principle of "subsidiarity" in the European Directive, which it was suggested

> would signify that the claimant would not necessarily be the person required to pay compensation to the *bona fide* possessor . . . [but] would be obliged to compensate the *bona fide* possessor only if compensation could not be obtained from another source[29].

While the discussion in the Committee of the Whole[30] canvassed two proposals in the same sense, they were not accepted. Certain delegations insisted that compensation should be an absolute right, not a conditional one. The reappearance in the final text, in a weakened form, of this provision which still leaves intact the right, rather than a mere claim, to compensation of the possessor returning the object, was the result of negotiations in the special working group.

Article 4(3)

> Payment of compensation to the possessor by the claimant, when this is required, shall be without prejudice to the right of the claimant to recover it from any other person.

---

25. Doc. 23 § 72.
26. Doc. 30 § 156, 175; Doc. 48 § 203.
27. Doc. 23 § 73; Doc. 30 §§ 62-63; Doc. 39 § 82.
28. Doc. 48 § 86.
29. Acts 183.
30. Acts 183 (Vrellis); 184 (Fraoua) 186-189, 286-292.

This clause does not seem to be necessary. It is difficult to see how payment of compensation by the claimant of an object to the person returning the object could adversely affect the claimant's right to recover it from some other person if the legal system already accorded such a right of recovery (for example, as against a thief or person otherwise held responsible for his loss).

The words "by the claimant" were dropped from the phrase "payment by the claimant of fair and reasonable compensation" in Article 4(1) at the Diplomatic Conference[31] and there was discussion of "subsidiarity" i.e. "that the claimant would not necessarily be the person required to pay compensation to the *bona fide* possessor but only obliged to compensate if compensation could not be obtained from another source"[32]. There therefore seems to be even less reason for this article.

A detailed proposal incorporating the principle of "subsidiarity" introduced by Turkey was strongly deprecated by a number of States and was defeated[33]. The present Article appeared in the compromise text prepared by the special working group. It seems clear that this was a hard fought compromise which has not in fact made the payment of compensation conditional on exhaustion of remedies against parties other than the claimant, though it would seems to authorise the claimant to join other parties in the action who may be liable for compensation[34].

Article 4(4)

> In determining whether the possessor exercised due diligence, regard shall be had to all the circumstances of the acquisition, including the character of the parties, the price paid, whether the possessor consulted any reasonably accessible register of stolen cultural objects, and any other relevant information and documentation which it could reasonably have obtained, and whether the possessor consulted accessible agencies or took any other step that a reasonable person would have taken in the circumstances.

The phrase "**due diligence**" was adopted over "necessary diligence" on the ground that if the object was subsequently found to have been stolen, then it was self-evident that the necessary diligence to prevent acquisition of a stolen object had *not* been exercised[35]. It would perhaps have been better to replace it by the phrase "required diligence" — not the degree of diligence required to prevent acquisition of a stolen object, but that *required* by the Convention, having due regard to the availability of information on the object. Unfortunately, "due diligence" is already a term of art in United States law, and would perhaps have been better avoided, as were the words "*bona fide*" and "equitable", in order to avoid confusion with existing terms of art. But this was not in all cases possible (see the discussion on "possessor" in Article 3(1)) and is not dangerous if the judges keep in mind that the term does not reflect existing domestic practice, but relates to the requirements of this Convention. The point was raised at the Diplomatic Conference which accepted the view of the Drafting Committee that "due diligence" was sufficiently clear[36].

31. Acts 183-189, 290-292.
32. Acts 183 (Vrellis).
33. Acts 292.
34. It appears to reflect Art. 11 of the European Directive which is, however, concerned with "illegally removed" (not stolen) cultural objects. Cf. discussion in Doc. 14 § 17 and Doc. 23 § 34 on Article 1(b) of Loewe preliminary draft (Doc. 3); the text of the Directive can be found in Appendix II.
35. Doc. 23 § 75.
36. Acts 289.

It was decided to give quite specific indicators of what was required[37]. The factors specified as examples in the test of diligence were settled, at the third meeting of the Study Group, as "the relevant circumstances of the acquisition, including the character of the parties and the price paid" together with the consultation of a register, leaving to the judge a discretion to decide which other factors he or she deemed to be relevant. The group did, however, insist that mention should be made in the explanatory report on the text of the factors mentioned in Article 7(2) and (3) of of LUAB[38] (the nature and provenance of the objects etc.). "Any special circumstances in respect of the transferor's acquisition of the object which are known to the possessor" should also be taken into account.

The phrase "**all the circumstances of the acquisition**" would cover factors such as an unusual place of the transfer (such as the bond area of an airport[39] or a trailer truck in a loading dock[40]) or time of day[41]. Undue haste to conclude the transfer would seem to indicate caution. Antiquities whose original container also revealed woodchips, soil and caterpillars[42] or mud and straw[43] must surely suggest the need for further inquiries. Some areas such as Afghanistan[44] or Iraq[45], which have been massively looted, have been well publicised: objects which might have such an origin need to be especially carefully scrutinised. Finally there are certain classes of antiquities where illicit origin should be presumed unless a clear chain of title can be shown.

> The known corpus of Cycladic figures is now reckoned at about 1600; a few are casual finds, about 143 have been recovered archaeologically; the other 1400 or so have . . . appeared on the market or in the possession of private collections inside or outside Greece with no declared recent history as to their movements between their places in the ground and the present proprietor. . . About 90 per cent of the corpus, then is practically without history . . .[46].

> In December 1985 large numbers of Apulian vases were offered sale at Sotheby's. A three volume publication of more than 6,000 Apulian vases listed every known and legally excavated vase from the area up to 1983. One or two might have been missed, but not more. None of those offered for sale were listed[47].

In such a case due diligence would require the dealer to seek proof that the objects were legally acquired.

A collector or dealer who wishes to acquire antiquities in a special corner of the market would be well advised to avoid an area where there is a 90 per cent chance of buying either an illegally excavated or fake object.

---

37. Doc. 23 §§ 76-78.
38. Draft LUAB cited p. 29, n. 3 Art. 7(3) and commentary of Sauveplanne thereon; Doc. 18 §§ 55-56, 60.
39. *Autocephalous Greek-Orthodox Church of Cyprus v. Goldberg & Feldman Fine Arts* Inc. 717 F.Supp. 1374 (1989); 917 F.2d 278 (1990) (U.S.).
40. D'Arcy, D. "The Sevso treasure: who did what and to whom" 31 *The Art Newspaper* October 1993 14, 38.
41. *Reid v. Metropolis Police Comr.* [1973] 2 All E.R. 97 (U.K.).
42. The copper cauldron holding the late Roman silver hoard known as "the Sevso treasure" as described in article cited n. 40 above, 38.
43. *United States v. McClain* 545 F.2d 988 (1977); 551 F.2d 52 (1977); 593 F.2d 658 (1979) (U.S.)
44. Press Release by UNESCO 30 March 1994; 65 *The Art Newspaper* December 1996 1-3; 66 January 1997, 6.
45. Press Release by UNESCO 4 March 1995, Notice of Stolen Cultural Property (UNESCO) 1 August 1995; *Lost Heritage: Antiquities Stolen from Iraq's Regional Museums*; Gibson, M. & McMahon, A. Fascicle 1 (Chicago 1993); Baker, H.D., Mathews, R.J. & Postgate, N. Fascicle 2 (Cambridge 1994); Fujii, H., Fascicle 3 (Tokyo 1996).
46. Chippindale, C. and Gill, D. "Cycladic figures: art versus archaeology?" in Tubb, K.W. *Antiquities Trade or Betrayed* 131 at 132.
47. *The Observer* 1 December 1985, 1; *The Times* 7 December 1985, 2, 10 December, 10

Recently the Swiss Federal Court held that the degree of care required from an acquirer varies according to the circumstances and has to be evaluated in each case. Certain classes of goods had already been held to be subject to particular risk, such as used luxury cars, where the buyer does not have to be alerted by particularly suspicious circumstances to make particular inquiries, but should be wary from the outset. The Court held that a heightened risk existed in the trade of second-hand goods generally and in all branches of the trade where goods of doubtful origin were particularly evident. This included antiquities[48] such as the antique weapons concerned in this case. This assessment of the circumstances is a realistic approach and virtually identical to the approach of Article 4(4) of the UNIDROIT Convention.

The "**character of the parties**" will be an important element in the judge's assessment of "due diligence". The big international auction houses have specialists in each area for the works that they sell. They would know as well as any museum conservator the best ways to check on provenance. Of them a high standard can be expected. Not to check a *catalogue raisonnée* of a major artist which would reveal prior ownerships clearly would not meet this standard. Specialised dealers also have particular knowledge of the art market which would enable them to suspect the origin of some cultural objects: those listed by INTERPOL or widely publicised in the general news media and in specialised publications, such as Malian ceramics[49] or cultural losses in massive quantities from Afghanistan[50] or Cambodia[51].

This is illustrated by a Swiss case following the legislation requiring the return of property stolen from occupied territories during World War II. Fischer, a dealer who had sold some valuable Impressionist paintings, had to reimburse the purchaser who was required to return them to their original owners. Swiss law, however, protected the *bona fide* purchaser, and the special legislation allowed a good faith purchaser, who could not recover from the seller, to be reimbursed by the Swiss State. When Fischer sued the State, however, he was awarded only about a third of the amount which he had had to reimburse the collector, since it held that he should, in the circumstances, have been more prudent. In coming to this conclusion, the court made a careful analysis of the transactions concerned. It held that, at the date of Fischer's purchases in 1941 and 1942, the illegal "confiscation" of Jewish property was not widely known and knowledge of it could not be imputed to him. In respect of paintings bought by him from the curator of Goering's collection, however, the court held that since the views of senior members of the Nazi party that the Impressionists were representatives of "degenerate" art were well known even before the war, the sudden appearance of large numbers of top quality Impressionist paintings for sale by Goering's curator should have put him on enquiry. His failure to make a full investigation as to provenance justified the granting of the reduced amount to him by the State.

---

48. *Versicherung X v. A.M.* ("Antique Weapons" case) BGE/ATF 122 III 1 (Federal Court Lausanne 5 March 1996) also reported in *Neue Zürcher Zeitung* 6/7 April 1996 41. For a recent very important English decision to the same effect, see Appendix XII. Cf. an assessment of factors in a United States decision, Appendix XIII.
49. Sidibe, S. "The Fight against the Plundering of Malian Cultural Heritage and Illicit Exportation" in Schmidt P.R. and McIntosh R.J. *Plundering Africa's Past* 1996, 79; Brent, M. "A View inside the Illicit Trade in African Antiquities" in same book, 63; ICOM *One Hundred Missing Objects from Africa; Looting in Africa* 1992 109-111; Bedaux, R. "An archaeologist's appeal" in Leyden, H. *Illicit traffic in cultural property: Museums against pillage* (Royal Tropical Institute, Amsterdam) 1995, 67-71; also the subject of an import ban imposed under the United States legislation implementing the 1970 UNESCO Convention cited p. 33, n. 43.
50. N. 44 above.
51. Widely publicised in the press and in ICOM, *100 Missing Objects: Looting in Angkor* 1st edition 1993, 2nd edition 1997.

(Even this may have been generous. Fischer had conducted a famous art auction for the Nazis in 1939 and might have been thought to have more insight into the activities of the Nazi authorities in the acquisition of art than most[52].)

Unfortunately, as Elisabeth des Portes, Secretary General of ICOM has pointed out

> It is evident that one can no longer rely on the fame of certain salerooms or dealers for assurance of the provenance of objects. The very efficient French Office pour la Répression de Vol des Oeuvres d'Art, which makes seizures both at the Hotel Drouot as well as at the big names of the market place, is there to prove it[53].

The offer, by the same person, of two very rare examples of a book by one of the survivors of the last voyage of Magellan, of which not more than ten copies exist in the entire world, and which were roughly disguised by the recent scratching out of several stamps, should have alerted a major auction house to a possible illegal transaction. According to evidence given before the French court the books had been published in Paris in 1575 and were offered to Sotheby's Paris which sold them on, although inquiries could have established that three copies of this book had been stolen during the 1970s from three French libraries, two of them in Paris[54]. Sufficient elements in this transaction exist to suggest that the level of diligence required by the UNIDROIT Convention would not have been met.

The Swiss Federal Court in the recent case concerning the antique weapons collection mentioned above took into account the fact that the transferee of some stolen antique weapons was not only a dealer with experience in second hand cars and real estate but a collector of antiquities and especially of old weapons. It was therefore justified to expect a higher degree of diligence from him[55].

Some major collectors, especially those who collect in defined categories, such as African art or Indian bronzes, particularly if they have had many years experience, can also be held to a high standard. Many of these major collectors have in fact professional advisers. What about smaller collectors and amateur buyers? Here the factors which should be known to experts or experienced buyers in the field cannot necessarily be attributed to them, although facts which are notorious, such as the massive losses mentioned, or the enormous illicit trade in icons, cannot be dismissed.

The best protection of the less than expert is the purchase from a reputable dealer on whose expertise he then relies. Reputable dealers at present repurchase items which they have sold which prove to be stolen. The "character of the parties" includes, therefore, reference to the character of the seller. A seller who has a police record, or with whom the purchaser has never previously dealt, or one who is selling objects completely outside his usual merchandise, or one who has no expertise at all in the subject, make it important for the purchaser to have made scrupulous inquiry into the provenance of the item.

The "**price paid**" is also an important consideration. If the price paid is substantially less than the market price, this already calls for inquiry. This does not preclude a reasonable bargain, but it

---

52. *Fischer v. Schweizerische Eidgenossenschaft* (unreported decision) Federal Court, Booty Chamber - 25 June 1952 discussed by Thilo, E. "La Restitution des Rapines de Guerre" 1 *Journal des Tribunaux* (1952) 386.
53. *Le Monde* 14 January 1997, 15.
54. Noce, V. *Libération* 15 September 1995, 28.
55. Case cited n. 48 above.

does mean that an acquirer must be satisfied that the low price is not due to the fact that there is a defect in the title. In a Swiss case, just decided, the First Public Law Court refused an appeal against the decision of the cantonal court to return to France a painting which was proved to have been stolen. The possessor in Switzerland sought to prevent return, alleging his good faith acquisition. The Federal Court noted that the purchaser in Switzerland had bought the painting, estimated at a value of 3,200,000 FF for 1,083,000 FF or 1,700,000 FF (the assertions of the purchaser varied), clearly, in either case, far below the value of the painting. The lower court, with whose assessment the Federal court saw no reason to interfere, noted also that the purchaser was an experienced businessman and connoisseur who had not concerned himself either with the authenticity or the provenance of the painting, who had in addition risked dealing with persons unknown and had not inquired into the legality of the importation of the painting into Switzerland[56].

Developments in the recording of stolen cultural objects led to the inclusion of "**any reasonably accessible register of stolen cultural objects**"[57]. Although computerized registers exist, there is not at present one consolidated data base. The IFAR-Art Loss Register is an important source of information not to be ignored. Police data bases, however, are not generally accessible by the public. UNESCO is co-operating with various bodies in the museum, informatics and police sectors, to help establish core data standards for the exchange of data and enhanced cooperation between existing data bases. It held a meeting on this subject at Prague in November 1996 with the support of the Getty Information Institute. The projected core data form, known as "Object ID", presented to a conference of collectors, dealers, insurers, appraisers, conservators and other cultural bodies organized at Amsterdam by the Getty Information Institute in May 1997, was unanimously supported. It will now be put into use by individuals and submitted to the governing bodies of UNESCO, ICOM and INTERPOL for endorsement as the international standard.

The words "**other relevant information and documentation which it could reasonably have obtained**" were inserted at the third meeting of Governmental Experts[58], and were intended to cover publications relevant to the objects such as excavation reports and duplicate museum catalogues. For example the Musée Guimet holds a duplicate catalogue for the Kabul Museum and the Ecole française de l'Extrême Orient holds one for the Angkor Conservation Centre: any buyer of objects which could have an Afghan or Khmer provenance would be well advised, considering the huge amounts of material looted from those two countries in recent unsettled conditions, to check such sources of information. A well-known publication of the mosaics of Cyprus was relevant in the case of the Kanakaria mosaics[59]. An excavation report of a dig in Afghanistan listed a rare, perhaps unique, Bodhisattva with garnet eyes. It was until recently with other finds of this excavation in the Jellalabad Museum, but is now in the Metropolitan Museum, New York[60]. The phrase would also cover computerised auction catalogues where these exist, either in a general data base such as "Thesaurus" or put on line by the auction houses themselves.

The closing phrase "**or took any other step that a reasonable person would have taken in the circumstances**" is clearly an answer to the exaggerated claim that it will be impossible to prove diligence. Judges in most legal systems are used to applying rules to determine what is reasonable

---

56 . L. v. Ordonnance rendu le 1er novembre par la Chambre d'accusation de Genève (the *Desportes Still-life* case) 1e Cour de Droit public, Decision of 1 April 1997.

57. Doc. 10 § 25; Doc. 14 §§ 30-35; Doc. 23 §§ 79-81.

58. Doc. 39 §§ 76-77.

59. Cited n. 39 above (U.S.).

60 Maier, T. "The Met digs in" *Newsday* (U.S.) 23 May 1995 B37-38.

in the circumstances, as is shown by the most recent Swiss case mentioned above. It is clearly wildly inaccurate to suggest that the Convention provides that

> Good faith is established only by "consulting every register of stolen artefacts all over the world. One must also establish if the goods need an export licence and if this is available. The dealer has the right to compensation only if he can prove that he has consulted every possible source[61]."

In general, the type of inquiries made should be adapted to the type of object concerned. It would be unwise to rely solely on searching a register of stolen cultural property when it is clear that the object is unlikely to have been registered: this is the case, for example, with cultural objects of African origin, since it is well known that there is a very low proportion of stolen cultural objects from that continent registered either with INTERPOL or with a commercial register. In such case excavation reports would be a much better source of information, and factors such as origin in a particular culture or community much more significant for checking[62]. Consulting the register is

> an additional precaution to be taken but it was not intended to signify that for the purchaser to be protected the object must be entered in a register[63].

Finally it should be noted that the description of the factors to be taken into account

> was not intended to be exhaustive but rather to offer a guide to judges without laying down strict legal rules[64].

Article 4(5)

The possessor shall not be in a more favourable position than the person from whom it acquired the cultural object by inheritance or otherwise gratuitously.

This article provides that a person who acquired the object gratuitously should not be in a more favourable position than the person from whom he had acquired it. A similar clause exists in the European Directive[65]. This provision meets the situation, not infrequently encountered in some countries, where a collector might buy an object, not unaware that its provenance was suspect, and gain tax advantages by donating it to a museum.

> Accepting donations of undocumented antiquities is one way that museums can circumvent their own acquisitions policies, which might otherwise prevent them from purchasing material of suspicious origin[66].

The experts thought it important not to allow this loophole to exist[67].

---

61. Barker, G. and Stewart L. "Maastricht — the last art fair?" *Daily Telegraph* 4 March 1996, quoting L.A. Lemmens, Secretary-General of TEFAF.
62. On due diligence of the buyer in general, and especially in the United States, see Pinkerton, L. 22 *Case Western Reserve Journal of International Law* (1990) 1, 16-20.
63. Doc. 14 § 30.
64. Explanatory Report § 67. Lalive, art. cited p. 32, n. 28, 39 points out that Art. 4(4) does not require extraordinary diligence, but only that reasonable degree of prudence already required by Swiss law and which is, moreover, already required by numerous ethical codes.
65. Doc. 18 §§ 63-67; Directive cited p. 38, n. 85 above Art. 9, para. 3. It should be noted that the Directive was based on one of the earlier drafts of the UNIDROIT Convention, though it subsequently diverged from it in some ways.
66. Elia, R. "The World cannot afford many more collectors with a passion for antiquities" 41 *The Art Newspaper* October 1994
67. Doc. 23 §§ 81-87.

ARTICLE 5

Articles 5-7 (Chapter III) deal specifically with illegal export and balance Articles 3-4 (Chapter II) which deal with stolen cultural property.

Professor Georges Droz, at a meeting organized by the Council of Europe at Delphi in 1983, first suggested providing for the return of an illegally exported cultural object without regulating the issue of ownership or transfer of title. Independently the same proposal had been made in the first draft of the scheme for the protection of the cultural heritage in the English-speaking countries in 1986 (see now Article 9(2), (3) and (4) of that scheme, Appendix VIII). A similar solution has been used in the Hague Convention on the Civil Aspects of International Child Abduction, 1980 - returning an abducted child as soon as possible to the country from which it had been abducted without first deciding the question of custody[1]. In both cases it is the physical presence on the territory and the refusal to give legal support to the wrongful action which are important, and resolution of the substantive legal questions should not delay the return.

A clause providing for the return of illegally exported cultural property appeared, like that of stolen cultural property, in the preliminary draft of Dr. Loewe[2]. Both categories were subject to limitations. The Study Group eventually abandoned restrictions on stolen cultural property, all of which must be returned. But it did not drop the limitations on illegally exported cultural property.

Dr. Loewe was convinced "that a considerable difference existed on the moral plane between theft and illicit export of cultural objects"[3] and it was clear that this view had traditionally been shared by many. Opponents of recognising foreign export controls speak of "retentionism"[4] or even "cultural nationalism"[5] thus making a moral judgment against a policy of export prohibition. But many export laws have highly moral purposes. For example, a State may seek to recover a cultural object illicitly exported to hand back to a tribal community which will itself have to resolve the question of rights to common property: New Zealand's effort to enforce export control was based on such a concern[6]. It may also wish to ensure return in cases where a custodian of traditional cultural property has been suborned to sell it against the traditions of a community and contrary to its wish[7], or to prevent exploitation of traditional communities who are given risible sums for material of considerable value. Contemporary evidence increasingly shows that prohibitions on export are used as a mechanism to deal with clandestinely excavated or otherwise wrongfully alienated cultural property. In these circumstances it does not seem appropriate to try to determine the refusal to apply foreign export controls as some kind of morally superior principle. There were, of course, many States who wanted all illegally exported objects returned[8].

---

1. Droz, art. cited p. 22, n. 4, § 11.
2. Doc. 3, Art. 4.
3. Doc. 10 § 33.
4. Merryman, p.20, n. 8; p. 23, n. 8 and related text.
5. Vernet, J. "Je suis allergique au nationalisme culturel" *Le Journal de Genève* 3 May 1996.
6. Case cited p. 32, n. 33; see discussion in text relating to p.59, n. 39.
7. See the examples given below, text relating to p. 58, nn. 35-36.
8. Doc. 30 §§ 77, 101, 116, 155, 169.

The Study Group understood the issue as one of assessing how far States would be prepared to give some kind of recognition to a foreign public law and it noted the doctrinal discussions which had recently taken place[9] and the more liberal attitudes which had been taken by the Convention of the European Communities on the Law Applicable to Contractual Obligations as well as Article 19 of the Swiss law on private international law and certain case law tending in the same direction[10]. There was general agreement that some recognition should be given to those rules, but there was also discussion of the fact that breach of export controls had not, until recently, been regarded by importing States as more than morally reprehensible, and that the number of illegally exported objects should, therefore, be limited[11] in order to ensure the widest possible acceptance of the Convention.

The criterion of commercial value was, however, seen as no more satisfactory in this connection than it had been in relation to stolen cultural property. Professor John Merryman then proposed a different approach: to limit return to those illegally exported cultural objects whose loss seriously impaired the cultural heritage of the State from which they were being exported[12]. This approach, refined and embellished, survived into the final text (now Art. 5(3)). Article 5(3) also restricted the number of items to be returned by language requiring some level of "significance". Finally Article 7 excluded two other classes of illegally exported cultural objects from the ambit of the Convention.

Article 5(1)

> A Contracting State may request the court or other competent authority of another Contracting State to order the return of a cultural object illegally exported from the territory of the requesting State.

Whereas it is the owner which can claim back stolen cultural property, it is the State from which an object has been illegally exported which has to request a court or other competent authority to return it. The First session of the Study Group already recognised the distinction between these two cases and it is clear that, where the owner had illegally exported, there may be an opposition of interests between the State and the owner.

It was admitted at an early stage that there could in some cases be an action either under Chapter II or Chapter III. A stolen object which has been legally exported (i.e. which is outside the categories of cultural objects whose export is controlled in the country of origin) will only be claimable under Chapter II. A stolen object which has been illegally exported can be claimed under either Chapter — this will apply to a clandestinely excavated object where, for example, all antiquities are vested in the State and subject to export control. An object which has not been stolen (but note that "stolen" may be interpreted more widely to cover fraud and conversion (Art. 10)) but has been illegally exported can be claimed only under Chapter III — this will apply where a cultural object has been illegally exported by its owner.

---

9. The Chairman of the Committee of the Whole at the Diplomatic Conference pointed out that the Institut de Droit international had adopted a Resolution some 20 years ago condemning the traditional view that foreign public laws should not be applied: Institut de Droit international, *Annuaire*, Session de Wiesbaden 1975 (Paris, 1975) 157.
10. Doc. 10 §§ 31-32. Detailed discussion of the position in legislation, conventions and case-law on this issue will be found in Prott, L.V. "Problems of Private International Law for the Protection of the Cultural Heritage", 217 *Recueil des Cours* (1989 - V) 219, 282-300.
11. Doc. 23 § 106-108; Doc. 30 §§ 95-96.
12. Doc. 10 Annex 4; Doc. 14 §§ 58-59.

The phrase "**court or other competent authority**" is used for the first time in this section. The words "or other competent authority" were added after discussion in the Study Group where it had been pointed out that some countries had vested jurisdiction in these kinds of matters in an administrative tribunal, and that a reference to courts alone could prevent them from acceding to a text which was otherwise acceptable[13]. Many States had adopted the UNESCO Convention scheme which was an administrative rather than court-based system[14]. It was also pointed out that this might enable a contracting State to provide a simpler and less expensive means of procedure than those normally available under the law[15] and that there were several options: a court of one or more judges, an *ad hoc* commission or even a mixed commission composed of both jurists and cultural experts[16].

A mechanism was proposed whereby a duly appointed central authority would be designated by each State at the time of the ratification of the Convention. This authority would centralise and transmit requests for return and communicate information[17]. Ultimately this reference to a "court or other competent authority" survived throughout the text, but a provision in Article 16 requires States to specify the procedure and competent bodies at the time of ratification.

A member of the Study Group explained that it was intentional that the present text was not more precise, and that a State was free to provide in its legislation implementing the Convention whether the action should be brought against a State or the possessor[18].

Article 5(2)

> A cultural object which has been temporarily exported from the territory of the requesting State, for purposes such as exhibition, research or restoration, under a permit issued according to its law regulating its export for the purpose of protecting its cultural heritage and not returned in accordance with the terms of that permit shall be deemed to have been illegally exported.

This article assimilates to illegal export the failure to return after legal export. It was inserted at the fourth meeting of Governmental Experts[19], probably with the inspiration of Article 2 of the European Directive. At that stage it was a much more complicated text which dealt with successive exports.

There has been some suggestion that this clause could make museums reluctant to organise international exhibitions relying on loan material, and lenders unwilling to lend it. It is difficult to see why this should be the case. The ICOM Code of Ethics provides that museums should not acquire any object which has been illegally exported from its country and/or any intermediate country in which it may have been legally owned (ICOM Article 3(2)) and that exhibitions should

---

13. Doc. 14 § 96 25; Doc. 18 § 71; Doc. 23 §§ 97-100; Doc. 30 §§ 81-82; Doc. 39 §§ 89-90; Acts 192-193, 199, 200-201, 202. See also the comments relating to Article 16.
14. Acts 192-193, 199.
15. Acts 200-201.
16. Acts 201.
17. Doc. 30 §§ 82-85; Doc. 39 §§ 89-90.
18. Doc. 30 § 84; Acts 200-203 (Fraoua).
19. Doc. 48, §§ 125-131, 136. In the draft which was considered at the Diplomatic Conference it was presented as Article 5(1)(b), Acts 15. Commentary of the UNIDROIT Secretariat, Acts 34 § 78; discussion at Acts 189 (Crewdson), 193 (Burman), 197 (Izadi), 199 (Izadi). It became Article 5(2) when renumbered by the Drafting Committee, Acts 336 and was unchanged in the compromise text.

be in accordance with the stated policy of the museum (of which this rule is clearly a part) (ICOM Article (3)). It would be natural for a museum which is to organise such an exhibition to seek information that the object concerned is being loaned by the owner or person otherwise qualified to deal with it, and to check the information as to export; indeed, this is required by the ICOM Code of Ethics (Art. 3(6)). If the proffered export certificate shows that the export is to be limited in time, then the museum is on notice that the object must be returned to the exporter or the country of export so that this condition can be complied with. If it is notified by the country of export of the lapse of time in respect of an object which, for some reason, it has in its possession unwittingly, it would have to return it. Where the lender disputes this then it would be normal for the museum to retain it while the competing claimants resolve the legal situation.

As far as lenders are concerned, consideration should be given to the statement of one of the participants at the Diplomatic Conference who shared

> . . . the general view that promotion and appropriate legal support for exhibitions abroad would be an effective step towards cultural relations among nations. He stressed that if States did not feel confident about the safe return of a cultural object sent to an exhibition, they would simply not participate[20].

It might be added that if a State does not feel confident that a condition as to temporary export in a licence will not be respected in another country, it is unlikely to grant the licence in the first place[21].

This provision raises the question of legislation which excludes the possibility of suing for the restitution of an object temporally within the country for exhibition. This issue already arises in relation to the European Directive. It will probably be necessary to make an exception to such legislation to enable compliance with the European Directive and the UNIDROIT Convention. Such an exception would of course be limited to cases arising under those two instruments and not necessarily extend to other cases such as nationalisation. (Mme. Shchuckin (French spelling Stchoukine) sued in France for the restitution of certain paintings, sent to Paris for exhibition, which had been expropriated from her father by the Russian State in the early days of the Revolution, a case which gave rise to the present French legislation on immunities in such circumstances[22].)

Article 5(3)

> The court or other competent authority of the State addressed shall order the return of an illegally exported cultural object if the requesting State establishes that the removal of the object from its territory significantly impairs one or more of the following interests:

The word "**establishes**" replaced the word "proves" which appeared in the early drafts[23]. The UNIDROIT Secretariat noted that the choice of the word "establishes" was a compromise between

---

20. Izadi, Acts 199.
21. On the question of temporary export licences generally see book cited p. 24, n. 23, 492-494.
22. Loi No. 94-679 du 8 août 1994 portant diverses dispositions d'ordre économique et financier Arts 60-61. *Stchoukine v. Le Centre national d'Art et de Culture Georges Pompidou, Le Musée de l'Eremitage de St. Petersbourg, Le Musée Pushkin de Moscou et la Fédération de Russie* TGI Paris, 1re Section, June 16 1993. See Redmond-Cooper, R. "Disputed Title to Loaned Works of Art: the Shchukin Litigation 1 *Art Antiquity and Law* (1996) 73.
23. Doc. 30 § 100-103; Doc. 39 § 107-112, 122-123; Doc. 48, 122.

those who wanted the automatic return of a cultural object for whom it would be sufficient to allege the impairment of the State's cultural heritage and those who would prefer the use of the stronger term "proves" to express the burden on the requesting State[24]. The United States representative stated that provision would not exclude the requested State from requiring such additional evidence as its courts might deem necessary[25]. The phrase "establishes" means that the judge must be satisfied that the object requested meets the tests of this article and judges in courts of location may take many factors into account in assessing whether that is the case. However courts are impartial and are also able to consider what kind of factors it is feasible for the requesting State to bring to its attention.

At the first session of the Study Group Professor Merryman had proposed, as an alternative to a criterion of pecuniary value, a list of essential interests in the preservation of the heritage[26]. They are now reflected in the text of this article.

The analysis of law in terms of interests is typical of United States doctrinal writings[27]. This kind of drafting is however less understood in other legal systems, though the antecedents of the theory are German[28] (and such analysis can still be found there[29]). In this Convention the impossibility of finding a conceptually satisfactory definition of the particular cases on which there was agreement made its utilitarian emphasis useful. During discussions by the Governmental Experts, it seemed clear that some would have felt more comfortable with a descriptive definition. This proved impossible to establish in a way which would achieve adequate support, and the formulation remained in the structure initiated in the Study Group[30].

Article 5(3)(a)

the physical preservation of the object or its context;

"the physical preservation of the object or of its context" would be impaired by physical damage to monuments and archaeological sites (including that done by illicit excavation, excavation without proper recording such as that in breach of the conditions of an excavation permit, or pillage) such as damage to Mayan stelae during their removal; spademarks, breaks and subdivision of materials; as well as physical damage to delicate objects by unprofessional handling by pillagers, possessors, runners, dealers etc. involved in the illicit export such as the cracking of paintings detached from their frames and the chipping of sculptures by inadequate packing;

---

24. Explanatory Report § 35.
25. Acts 298-299.
26. Doc. 10 §§ 38-39.
27. Due to the influence of Roscoe Pound (1870-1964) at Harvard and as restated by Julius Stone (1907-1985) *Social Dimensions of Law and Justice* (1966).
28. von Heck, P. (1858-1943) *Gestezauslegung und Interessenjurisprudenz* (1914); *Begriffsbildung und Interessenjurisprudenz* (1932). A bibliography of the German school is included in Stone, J. *Legal Systems and Lawyers' Reasonings* (1964) 228.
29. See, for example, Wyss M.P. "Rückgabeansprüche für illegal ausgeführte Kulturgüter" in Fechner *et al.* book cited p. 23, n. 9, 204-206.
30. Discussed Doc. 14 §§ 58-59; Doc. 30 §§ 97-98, 101; Doc. 39 §§ 105-112; Doc. 48 §§ 118-119.

Article 5(3)(b)

the integrity of a complex object;

"the integrity of a complex object" would be impaired by the dismemberment of complex objects such as the beheading of Khmer sculptures, removal of a façade of a Mayan temple; dispersion of frescoes, division of triptyches, or stripping interiors from historic buildings[31];

Article 5 (3)(c)

the preservation of information of, for example, a scientific or historical character;

"the preservation of information of, for example, a scientific or historical character" would be impaired by the loss of information by removal of objects from their context and irreversible damage to the context such as disturbance of stratigraphy by use of earth moving equipment or clandestine excavation; the break-up of a collection through misappropriation from a museum or the loss of documentation by destruction of an inventory etc.

After the adoption of Article 3(2) the question arose as to its relation to Article 5(3)(c). By virtue of the fact that a number of States expressly provide, in their national law, that archaeological objects are State property, they could already have proceeded under Article 3 as owner of a stolen cultural object. To do so, however, they would have to be able to precisely identify the object, which, by nature of its emergence into contemporary cultural life, was likely to be very difficult to do. But they could also proceed under Article 5, on the basis that the object has been illicitly exported, and if the relevant legislation on export control uses a generic description, such as "all pre-Columbian antiquities" and the loss "significantly impairs" the cultural heritage, then the obligation to return would be clear.

The adoption of Article 3(2) muddied this clear position although, by the adoption of the words "when consistent with the law of the State where the excavation took place" in that article, it may come to the same thing. Discussion at the fourth meeting of Governmental Experts[32] resulted in the insertion in square brackets of yet another subclause in Article 5 which required the return of a cultural object which has been taken from a site contrary to the laws of the requesting State applicable to the excavation of cultural objects and removed from that State.

Despite the efforts of many representatives at the Diplomatic Conference to explain that this created unnecessary confusion in the text and could indeed be harmful[33], it was retained by the Committee of the Whole although Article 3(2) and Article 5(3)(c) both remained. However it was dropped from the compromise text finally adopted[34].

---

31. It should be noted that the inclusion of the words "monument or archaeological site" in Art. 3(4) now provide a longer period of limitation for many such objects which can be proved to have been stolen.
32. Doc. 48 §§ 109-115, 137-140.
33. Doc. 48 §§ 138-140; Acts §§ 190-194, 292, 294 (then numbered 5(1)ter).
34. Doc. 48 §§ 109-115.

Article 5(3)(d)

the traditional or ritual use of the object by a tribal or indigenous community,

"the traditional or ritual use of the object by a tribal or indigenous community" is impaired by removal of important cultural objects from the control of the community such as the textiles from the peoples of Coroma, Bolivia, which they believed embodied the spirits of their ancestors from whom they would request guidance for the community[35]; traditional carvings representing spirits, ritual objects such as masks in traditional communities, funerary objects, stones which represent spirits and the connection of an individual to the land such as the *tjuringas* of Australian Aborigines[36]. It is not essential that the object actually be physically within the community to fall within this category: the removal of a sacred object from a museum or keeping-place or other collection to which it had been lent or was kept with the consent of the traditional authorities, (for example for security, or conservation) and which was under their control, and could be used for ceremonies when they wished, would also fall within this clause.

The variety of the objects given as examples indicates how difficult it would be to find a purely descriptive definition of the objects to be covered. Any object the removal of which could be argued to involve damage of any of the kinds specified should therefore be returned in order to deter damaging activities of the types listed.

In choosing these four categories of interest the article chooses situations which involve a loss not only to the cultural community which has lost the object, but also to humanity as a whole. The destruction and damage of cultural objects, the dismemberment of sites, the loss of contextual information which destroys historical knowledge of importance to the story of human development and the destruction of a living cultural tradition are all losses which impoverish the culture of all of us.

The UNIDROIT Secretariat has also pointed out that the interests are alternative and not cumulative and the list is not strictly exhaustive, since a State may decide under Article 10 to apply any rules more favourable to the return of illegally exported cultural objects than those provided by the Convention[37]. This applies to countries like Australia and Canada which have, in their legislation implementing the 1970 UNESCO Convention, agreed to return all cultural objects illegally exported from other States.

The requesting State has to establish that the removal of the object from its territory has impaired one of the interests listed in Article 5(3) (a) to (d). An object which has been damaged in transit, clandestinely excavated, dismembered, or removed from a traditional community clearly will meet that test. But what if the object has been for 30 years in private ownership before the illegal export? Does its removal from the country still significantly impair one of these interests? (The damage has been done long before.)

---

35. The subject of a Canadian prosecution of a dealer in *R. v. Yorke* Decision of the Supreme Court of Nova Scotia 20 June 1996 CR 11741 (not yet reported); Bomberry, V., "Organizing the Return of the Sacred Textiles to the Community of Coroma, Bolivia" 1993 *Akwe:kon Journal* 2.
36. For information on the legal and spiritual significance of *tjuringas*, see the discussion in Prott & O'Keefe, book cited p. 24, n. 23, 870, 883-884.
37. Explanatory Report § 35.

In such cases the courts will have to proceed on the basis of the specific evidence brought in each individual case in order to take its decision. For example it could be argued that the illegal export of an object which formed part of a significant historical collection would impair the preservation of information of a historical character by the separation out of the collection of one of its integral components. And the removal of an object which is an integral part of regalia or ritual objects of a traditional community may destroy the information which the assemblage as a whole provides. Each case will have to be examined on its merits.

> or establishes that the object is of significant cultural importance for the requesting State.

The predecessor of the phrase "or establishes that the object is of significant cultural importance for the requesting State" was proposed by the writer at the same time as the "Merryman list"[38] in order to cover some notable cases which may not fall precisely under one of the four heads given above. Such a case was that of *Attorney-General of New Zealand v. Ortiz*[39], where the New Zealand government failed to obtain the return to it of important Maori carvings which had been illegally exported from New Zealand and were to be auctioned at Sotheby's in London. The carvings had been buried for safekeeping by the tribe last century, when under attack, up until the time when they were extracted by the seller. They were sold by him to the dealer who illegally exported them. Of a style no longer being practised (the Taranaki style) and of extremely fine technique and beauty, the New Zealand government wanted to use them as an inspiration to young Maori carvers. Would a court accept that their loss affected their traditional or ritual use by a tribal or indigenous community? Although the New Zealand government wanted to use the carvings to promote and revive traditional cultural skills, that had not been done before the time of the illegal export. Nevertheless there is little doubt that the New Zealand government could have proved that these panels were of great cultural importance to the New Zealand people. Case-law will determine what sort of evidence will be needed and how hard it will be to prove this element. The case is so far unique, but such is the nature of cultural works that it seemed wise to make allowance for such unusual cases in the Convention. Fraoua points out that such cases will be relatively rare[40]. This clause is not likely, therefore, to substantially enlarge the ambit of the section.

A further consideration may be the need of every State to have at least a representative collection of its own outstanding cultural achievements[41]. Where all other examples of works representing a particularly important cultural tradition have already been removed from the country, the export of the last example would obviously fall within the scope of this phrase.

One misunderstanding which has been expressed is that an "exporting" State was being given the right to declare any object whatever to be "significant"[42]. This is not the case: if a requesting State claims the object before a court or other tribunal in the requested country it has to prove, to the satisfaction of the tribunal, that the object is of great cultural importance[43]. This it can do by

---

38. Doc. 10 § 40.
39. Cited above p. 32, n. 33.
40. Fraoua, R. art. cited p. 15, n. 1, 323.
41. See p. 24, n. 23 and related text.
42. Fitzpatrick, J. art. cited p. 10, n. 10, 20. See the vigorous rejection of this view by Lalive, P. article cited p.13, n. 7, 56 and, in more detail, his art. cited p. 32, n. 28, 45-46.
43. Doc. 18 § 69; Doc. 48 § 122; Lalive, art. cited p. 32, n. 28, 48

bringing evidence of art historians, anthropologists etc. as New Zealand could well have done in the case concerning the Taranaki panels. The suggestion that it would be practically impossible for a private litigant "to disprove" a claim by a foreign cultural minister that an object is "of significant cultural importance" shows little appreciation of the independence and impartiality of the judiciary in States evaluating such claims.

It is also evident that no State is likely to request an object, given the cost of litigation in "art market" States, and the difficulties of operating in another language and another legal system, unless the object really is of outstanding importance[44].

What is **significant cultural importance**? The original proposal for this phrase in the Study Group was "of great importance"[45]. This was amended within the group to "of outstanding cultural importance". The word "significant" was substituted for "outstanding" at the Diplomatic Conference after strong debate in the working group which finally put together the compromise text adopted at the end of the conference. One may ask whether the phrase "significant . . . importance" really has any meaning, and in any case, how it relates to "significantly impairs". The eleventh hour cobbling of the compromise package did not allow the drafting committee to work on the text and it will be left to national legislatures and to judges to work out exactly what it means. In order to make sense of the provision, it may be necessary to understand the word "significant" in the sense of "great", which certainly would provide a more comprehensible English expression.

It is clear, even from the drafting of the article, that the final clause is a fifth (alternative) category of greater cultural importance than those listed in (a), (b), (c) and (d)[46]. Their removal has only to "significantly impair" one of the interests mentioned, whereas the final alternative has to establish that the object *itself* is of a high degree of importance — perhaps less than outstanding, but certainly more than "significant" or "important" ("**significant** cultural **importance**").

Though some experts wanted to make *all* illegally exported cultural objects, without exception, subject to the obligation of return[47], others made it clear that their countries would not accept such an obligation[48]. Some members of the Study Group, and also some of the Governmental Experts, were not particularly happy about the final clause which they thought broadened too much the class of objects which could be recovered[49]. If understood as described in the last paragraph, this should not be the case. However, they had suggested, as an alternative, the substitution of "and" for "or", thus making the phrase "of outstanding significance" an additional qualification of the four criteria already set out[50]. This view was rejected at the fourth meeting of Governmental Experts[51] and an attempt to reintroduce it was rejected by the Diplomatic Conference[52].

The principle behind the limited recognition of export restrictions was discussed hotly at a number of the meetings, most significantly at the second meeting of Governmental Experts[53] and was

---

44. A list of the difficulties faced by such claimants is graphically described in Walden, D.A. "Canada's Cultural Property Export and Import Act: the Experience of Protecting Cultural Property" *University of British Columbia Law Review* Special Issue (1995) 203, 214-126.
45. Doc. 10 § 40; Doc. 14 §§ 59-61; Doc. 18 §§ 78-79; Doc. 48 §§ 120-121.
46. Doc. 48 § 124.
47. Doc. 23 §§ 106-114; Doc. 30 § 77; Doc. 39 § 100; Acts 194 (Bombogo).
48. Doc. 23 §§ 107-108; Doc. 39 § 102; Acts 194.
49. Doc. 23 § 110 (cf. 155).
50. Acts 196, 198.
51. Doc. 48, 142-144.
52. Acts 194-203, 294-297.
53. Doc. 23 §§ 90-93, 106-110; Doc. 30 §§ 77-79, 94-103; Doc. 39 § 97.

raised again at the Diplomatic Conference[54]. However the issue emerged from the working group of the Diplomatic Conference which produced the compromise draft with the restriction intact and it is clear that a substantial number of States felt the form of provision now in Article 5 stretched to the outer limit of possible acceptance by their States.

Article 5(4)

> Any request made under paragraph 1 of this article shall contain or be accompanied by such information of a factual or legal nature as may assist the court or other competent authority of the State addressed in determining whether the requirements of paragraphs 1 to 3 have been met.

The Loewe preliminary draft (Appendix II) included conditions for return and these were discussed at many points in the negotiations. They had at times covered factors such as non-confiscation, public access, security and so on[55]. After the third meeting of the Study Group the comparable article read:

> To be admissible, any request made under the preceding paragraph shall contain, or be accompanied by, the particulars necessary to enable the competent authority of the State addressed to evaluate whether the conditions laid down in paragraph (3) are fulfilled and shall contain all material information regarding the conservation, security and accessibility of the cultural object after it has been returned to the requesting State[56].

A number of experts were uneasy at this formulation and some found confusion as to whether the conditions were of admissibility or substance. The reasoning behind the article was explained: the desire to enhance the credibility of the requesting State by asking it to motivate the request for return by demonstrating the significant cultural interest of the object and not only the fact that it belonged to its national heritage. The second reason was the psychological effect which the provision might have on the requesting State which would be obliged to take the necessary steps to ensure the protection of the cultural object whose return it was requesting[57]. Despite some sympathy for these ideas and much discussion[58], the idea of admissibility was finally dropped by the fourth meeting of Governmental Experts[59] and the article did not receive much discussion at the Diplomatic Conference[60].

The replacement of the reference to "conservation, security and accessibility" by "such information of a factual or legal nature as may assist . . . in determining whether the requirements of paragraphs 1 to 3 have been met" probably now eliminates the need to consider conditions of "conservation, security and accessibility".

---

54. Acts 192, 194-203, 294-297.
55. Doc. 10 §§ 44-47; Doc. 14 §§ 66-68; Doc. 18 §§ 91-94.
56. Discussion reported in Doc. 18 §§ 91-94; Doc. 23 §§ 101-105; Doc. 30 § 115; Doc. 39 §§ 92-96; Doc. 48 §§ 116-117, 141.
57. The elements which would be appropriately included in the assessment of these factors were proposed to the second meeting of experts in Doc. 13, 2-4.
58. Doc. 30 §§ 86-94.
59. Doc. 48 § 116-117.
60. Acts 298-299.

Article 5(5)

Any request for return shall be brought within a period of three years from the time when the requesting State knew the location of the cultural object and the identity of its possessor, and in any case within a period of fifty years from the date of the export or from the date on which the object should have been returned under a permit referred to in paragraph 2 of this article.

The previously different periods of limitation for claims of stolen cultural property and illegally exported cultural objects were finally aligned at the fourth meeting of Governmental Experts[61]. The relevant issues concerning the limitation periods have all been discussed above in connection with Article 3(3). It is to be noted, however, that there is no exceptional extension, as in Articles 3(4)-(8), for articles of a particular origin (monuments, public collections, traditional and indigenous communities)[62]. It is interesting to note that for the Member countries of the European Union, accepting the UNIDROIT Convention will ensure that the same rules apply to public collections subject to theft as to those subject to illicit removal under the European Directive (Article 7(2)). It would seem anomalous to allow more generous limitation periods in the case of illegal export than for theft, but this will be the case for States subject to the European Directive which do not become party to the UNIDROIT Convention.

---

61. Doc. 18 §§ 87-88; Doc. 30 §§ 144-148, 151; Doc. 48 §§ 171-172, 184.
62. Doc. 39 § 153, Acts, 203-207, 300-301.

ARTICLE 6

Article 6(1)

> The possessor of a cultural object who acquired the object after it was illegally exported shall be entitled, at the time of its return, to payment by the requesting State of fair and reasonable compensation, provided that the possessor neither knew nor ought reasonably to have known at the time of acquisition that the object had been illegally exported.

The principle of compensating a person who has to return an illegally exported cultural object was also hard fought[1]. It is important to note that only a person acquiring an illegally exported cultural object after the date of export is entitled to compensation. An owner who knowingly arranges the illicit export of a cultural object covered by Article 5(3) is not entitled to compensation. Note that a dealer may be liable for breach of a warranty of quiet possession, if a claim for return is made out[2].

The phrase "**knew or ought reasonably to have known**" was chosen to align the text with Article 4(1)[3] although other alternatives ("should at least have had doubts"[4], "purchaser on notice"[5], absence of certificate would raise an irrebuttable presumption of bad faith[6]) had been proposed.

The phrase "**at the time of its return**" is parallel to the phrase "at the time of restitution" in Article 4(1). Although one speaker thought that the possessor of an unlawfully exported object should be entitled to refuse to return the object until the compensation had been received[7], and a representative of the art trade even suggested that the market value of the object should be deposited prior to the institution of proceedings "as a precaution against vexatious law suits"[8], (a provision which would surely have totally precluded action by developing States), the Diplomatic Conference preferred not to deal with this in detail in the text and to leave it to the judge to find the appropriate arrangements for payment.

The phrase "**payment by the requesting State**" was retained in Article 6(1) although the parallel phrase "payment by the claimant" was dropped in Article 4(1)[9].

Article 6(2)

> In determining whether the possessor knew or ought reasonably to have known that the cultural object had been illegally exported, regard shall be

---

1. Doc. 23 §§ 135-137; Doc. 30 §§ 154-155; Doc. 39 §§ 160-163; Acts 217-218.
2. Cf. p.42, n. 11 and related text.
3. Doc. 23 §§ 135-138; Doc. 48 § 192.
4. Doc. 3, Art 4(1) predecessor of Art. 6(2) on illicit export, discussed Doc. 14 §70.
5. Doc. 38, Misc. 7; Acts 218-222.
6. Doc. 39 § 166; Doc. 38 Misc. 7.
7. Acts 216 (Nomura).
8. Acts 217 (Gaiser).
9. See the discussion on Article 4(2) and 4(3).

> had to the circumstances of the acquisition, including the absence of an
> export certificate required under the law of the requesting State.

Whereas a judge deciding whether the acquirer of a stolen cultural object who has to return it will
have regard

> to all the circumstances of the acquisition, including the character of the parties, the price
> paid, whether the possessor consulted any reasonably accessible register of stolen cultural
> objects, and any other relevant information and documentation which it could reasonably
> have obtained, and whether the possessor consulted accessible agencies or took any other
> step that a reasonable person would have taken in the circumstances (Art. 4(4))

the judge considering whether the possessor knew or ought reasonably to have known at the time
of acquisition that the object had been illegally exported will have regard to

> the circumstances of the acquisition, including the absence of an export certificate required
> under the law of the requesting State.

While this formulation does not exclude reference to the same factors as those applicable in the case
of a stolen cultural object[10], the failure to mention them specifically does suggest that the standard of
care in respect of stolen cultural objects is higher than that required in respect of illicit export.

Dr. Loewe's preliminary draft provided for compensation in all cases for the return of illegally
exported cultural property[11] (or, in the alternative, retaining the ownership but returning the
object to the country of export, as is still now provided in Article 6(3)). The Study Group,
however, decided to make compensation dependent on some degree of care on the part of the
returning party[12] and the Governmental Experts were of the same view[13].

The fourth meeting of experts received a proposal which would have aligned the diligence requirements
of Article 6(1) with those of 4(1)[14]. The discussion became involved with another draft article
which, in its original form (Article 8bis) would have required States to implement a system of export
certificates[15] and was subsequently rephrased to make the absence of an export certificate, where one
was required, as evidence of knowledge of the acquirer[16]. The Diplomatic Conference chose to
adopt the present formulation, which was proposed as a compromise by the Swiss Delegation and
incorporated the reference to the export certificate into the text of Article 6(1). This was one of the
articles agreed on by the working group as part of the compromise package[17].

The phrase "due diligence" does not appear. Nevertheless, in considering whether the acquirer
"knew or ought reasonably to have known . . . that the object had been illegally exported" the
judge may well look to the factors discussed in relation to Article 4(4) above[18].

---

10. Doc. 23 §§ 135-139; Doc. § 158.
11. Doc. 3, Art. 5.
12. Doc. 10 § 43; Doc. 14 § 69; Doc. 18 §§ 96-101.
13. Doc. 23 §§ 135-138; Doc. 30 §§ 154-155, 158; Doc. 39 §§ 159-163, 167-168.
14. Doc. 48 §§ 188-190. Cf. Doc. 39 § 182.
15. Proposal of Iran, Doc. 30 §§ 75-76; Doc. 39 §§ 39, 91, 166; Doc. 48 §§ 47, 91-99, 132, 194-200, 209. Cf. The
    provision of a "validation certificate" in the Commonwealth Scheme Appendix VIII Art. 4, reflecting currrent museum
    practice seeking information from the possible States of export; failure to reply precludes a claim by the exporting
    State but failure by an acquirer to use the validation system results in presumption against innocent purchase.
16. Acts 103.
17. Acts 216-222, 305.
18. See also Pinkerton, art. cited p. 51, n. 62, 20-25; cf. Commonwealth Scheme, Appendix VIII Art. 9(3) "due care
    and attention".

What kinds of circumstances are then relevant in testing whether compensation is appropriate for an acquirer who has to return an illicitly exported cultural object? The cases already give some indication. When George Ortiz bought the Taranaki panels from the dealer Lance Entwhistle, he signed a contract of sale in New York which included a clause obliging him not to show the panels to any archaeologist of New Zealand extraction for two years nor to entrust a photograph of them to any third party[19]. There can be no doubt that compensation would be excluded by Article 6(1) in such a case. In *R v Yorke*, the judge had this to say:

> Yorke was . . . in the process of publishing a book on Aymara weavings to come out in April of 1988. From all the documentation and from his own demeanour and questions, publications, correspondence, it is very apparent that the accused is extremely knowledgeable about the weavings. . . .

> . . . the accused conducted a portion of the cross-examination. His questions on cross-examination were lengthy and frequently amounted to an exposition rather than a question. By these questions he displayed his extensive knowledge of Bolivia, its government , its indigenous people, its culture and weavings. His discussions . . . were extremely enlightening on this vast knowledge of the textile industry.

> I would find that the accused had a wealth of knowledge about native history and culture. He had a reliable business practice for recording and describing in detail his collection of antique weavings . . . The business-like manner with which the accused went about collecting, cataloguing, detailed descriptions and his business connections in Bolivia indicate that the accused was or should have been aware of the laws and regulations pertaining to this industry[20].

It is sometimes said that it is impossible to find out whether an object is subject to export control or not. The export control laws have been summarized in a study for UNESCO and are available free of charge[21] and UNIDROIT is planning to put them on line so that they will always be up to date. In some cases there can be no question that export controls apply: all of the countries which were once included within the boundaries of the Roman Empire have export controls on antiquities of major importance such as the Sevso treasure, which must have come from one of those countries[22]. Two rare books published in Paris in 1525 and offered in Paris to the branch of Sotheby's there, which must have known of the French rules requiring export permits for cultural objects of such value, were transferred for sale to Sotheby's New York, apparently without any consideration of the breach of the law[23]. More recently the Milan "old paintings" expert of the same auction house was filmed offering to arrange exportation of a painting from Italy to London (which subsequently occurred), not only with evident knowledge that this was breaking the law of the country in which he lived, but also clearly as part of a consistent practice[24].

With regards to "**fair and reasonable compensation**", this was aligned with the provision in Article 4(1) over an alternative provision for "the price paid by the possessor" proposed by members

---

19. Case cited p. 32, n. 33 above. Details from Cater, R.R. "The Taranaki Panels — a case study in the recovery of cultural heritage" 34 *Museum* (1982) 256.
20. Cited p. 58, n. 35, Decision 11-12.
21. O'Keefe, P.J. & Prott, L.V. Study cited p. 12, n. 2 above.
22. P. 47, nn. 40, 42.
23. Case cited p. 49, n. 54 above.
24. Watson P. *Sotheby's: The Inside Story* (London, 1997) 10-50. The book was serialised in *The Times* beginning 6 February 1997.

of the group who felt that a good faith acquirer of an illegally exported cultural object should in all cases receive full reimbursement[25]. "Market value" was also mentioned[26]. The group thought that "fair and reasonable compensation" would allow a judge to take all the circumstances into account[27]. There was relatively little detailed discussion of the measure of compensation at the Diplomatic Conference, since this had been thoroughly discussed in relation to Article 4(1)[28].

Article 6(3)

> Instead of compensation, and in agreement with the requesting State, the possessor required to return the cultural object to that State, may decide:
>
> (a)   to retain ownership of the object; or
>
> (b)   to transfer ownership against payment or gratuitously to a person of its choice residing in the requesting State who provides the necessary guarantees.

The origin of this article was a provision in the Loewe preliminary draft (Appendix II) that a possessor required to return an illegally exported object could opt either for compensation "or transfer the property, for reward or gratuitously, to a person of his choice in the requesting State". In the latter case, the requesting State would undertake not to confiscate the property nor interfere with its possession in any other way[29]. The Study Group noted that the penalty for illegal export by an owner was, in certain countries, the forfeiture of the object concerned and some thought that, in imposing return, the Convention should not endorse what was in effect a confiscation by the requesting State[30]. Others thought that the adoption of a minimum set of uniform rules of an essentially private law character should not be seen as interfering with the working of the criminal or administrative law of another State[31]. Article 6(3)(a) therefore allows the person returning the object to retain his ownership of it. States may therefore have to examine the wording of their provisions concerning forfeiture of objects which have been the subject of an illegal export (noting, of course, that an illegally exporting owner will not itself have the benefit of this Article 6(3)).

A further concern was expressed that, where an owner had already illegally exported, return to a person of his choice might simply be an invitation to evade the law again e.g. by enabling him or her to re-export illegally — but to a country not party to the UNIDROIT Convention[32]. So the words **"in agreement with the requesting State"** were added[33].

The article in its present form was considered to be also of advantage to the requesting State. If the requesting State should be unable to pay compensation, it could at least come to some arrangement with the person returning the object, which could thus be returned to the territory of that State, even though the State did not have the resources to offer compensation[34].

---

25. Doc. 14 §§ 77, 86-89; cf. also Doc. 18 § 101; Doc. 23 § 135; Doc. 39 § 135; Acts 216.
26. Acts 217-218.
27. Doc. 18 § 101.
28. Acts 216-217, 305.
29. Doc. 3 Art. 5.
30. Doc. 10 § 48; Doc. 14 §§ 16, 51, 78-79.
31. Doc. 10 § 48; Doc. 14 §§ 51, 79; Doc. 18 § 99.
32. Doc. 18 § 100.
33. Added at the second meeting of experts Doc. 14 §§ 78-81, explained at the third, Doc. 18 §§ 99-100, 102-103. This clause was also discussed at Doc. 23 §§ 141-145; Doc. 30 §§ 159-166, Doc. 39 §§ 171-174, Doc. 48 § 201.

A proposal was made for payment by another person of compensation in relation to illegally exported cultural objects similar to that accepted for stolen cultural property, but it was defeated[35]. On the other hand, nothing in the Convention prevents another source contributing the necessary funds.

Article 6(3)(b) therefore allows the owner the option of transferring ownership of the object to a person resident in the country to which it is returned (for example, he or she may decide to donate, lend or sell it to a museum in the country concerned). The provision does not, however, interfere with the property law of the country to which it is returned; the provision is designed only to ensure that the object is physically returned to the country of export, not to settle ownership issues[36].

The person to whom the object is transferred has to be someone "**who provides the necessary guarantees**". The State may thus ensure that the nominee meets minimal requirements of security and conservation for the object concerned[37].

Article 6(4)

> The cost of returning the cultural object in accordance with this article shall be borne by the requesting State, without prejudice to the right of that State to recover costs from any other person.

The question of the cost of return was not debated after the third meeting of the Governmental Experts[38]. Introduced after the second meeting of the Study Group[39] some experts thought it not necessary to mention the cost of return, as this was one of the factors which the judge would need to assess in determining what was "fair and reasonable". In any event the requesting State would already have incurred substantial expenses including those of the proceedings and perhaps the payment of compensation[40]. There is no parallel provision in respect of stolen cultural objects, and it will therefore be open to a judge to decide where these costs should fall in the case of stolen objects. The cost of return is one of the expenses which could be covered by any fund which might be established (see commentary on Article 4(1)). It can, however be argued that, even though this is specifically mentioned as a cost for the returning State, the amount likely to be necessary, along with the expenses already undertaken and the availability or not of a fund, should be taken into account by the judge. This approach reflects that of the Commonwealth Scheme which, while providing that the country of export may be required to meet the expense of return, where these are of an extraordinary nature the two States will consult on terms and conditions (Appendix VIII Art. 16).

Reimbursement of restoration costs was mentioned by the Japanese Delegation at the Diplomatic Conference, but this suggestion, as in the case of Article 4(1), was not incorporated into the text by the Diplomatic Conference[41].

---

34. Doc. 39 §§ 171-172; Acts 222-223; 306-307.
35. Doc. 30 § 156, 175; Doc. 48 § 203.
36. Acts 222-223, 306-307.
37. Doc. 18 §§ 100, 102-103; Doc. 23 §§ 141-145; Doc. 30 § 171.
38. Doc. 39 § 175-177; Doc. 48 § 202; Acts 223.
39. Doc. 18 §§ 106-110.
40. Doc. 18 § 106; Doc. 23 § 145; Doc. 30 §§ 167, 43; Doc. 39 § 175.
41. Doc. 30 §§ 155, 170, Doc. 39 § 170; Acts, 216. See discussion relating to pp. 43-44, nn. 17-22.

The phrase "**without prejudice to the right of that State to recover costs from any other person**" is an element reflecting the concern that a wrongdoer should be forced to pay rather than the requesting State[42] and is roughly parallel to Article 4(2) and (3).

Article 6(5)

> The possessor shall not be in a more favourable position than the person from whom it acquired the cultural object by inheritance or otherwise gratuitously.

This article is exactly parallel to Article 4(5) (see commentary above) and was inserted during the third session of the study group[43] to ensure parallel consideration under Chapter II and Chapter III.

---

42. Doc. 30 § 155.
43. Doc. 18 §§ 97, 111; Doc. 39 § 178. Cf. Commonwealth Scheme Appendix VIII, Art. 9(3) "innocent purchaser for value".

ARTICLE 7

Article 7(1)

The provisions of this Chapter shall not apply where:

The provisions of Article 5(3) clearly cut the number of cultural objects which would be returned after illicit export below that which would be liable to be returned after theft. Nonetheless there were some additional factors which it was felt should be taken into account.

(a)   the export of a cultural object is no longer illegal at the time at which the return is requested; or

Article 7(a) deals with the case where export is no longer illegal at the time of the action. It was inserted at the third session of the Study Group on the ground that national rules governing export are subject to change and that there would be little virtue in a State depriving one of its own citizens of an object which, on return, could immediately be legally re-exported[1].

(b)   the object was exported during the lifetime of the person who created it or within a period of fifty years following the death of that person.

Section (b) concerns an export which took place during the lifetime of the creator. It was argued that export should not be hindered in such cases since the development of an overseas market or the free sale of a person's creative work acts as an encouragement to further creative activity: this provision would ensure that there would be relatively no interference with the careers of professional artists, many of whom are dependent on recognition outside their own country to establish their reputations[2]. At various stages different periods were suggested - 5 years (sufficient time to enable the winding up of the estate)[3], 20 years (based on some national legislation[4] or as a compromise[5]), 50 years (based on the Convention for the Creation of an International Union for the Protection of Literary and Artistic Works 1886 (Berne Convention[6])[7] and the European Directive) and even 100 years[8]. The Diplomatic Conference settled for 50 years[9]. The rule is more generous than that presently applied in the United Kingdom. In 1994 the British authorities refused an export licence for a painting by Lucien Freud[10].

The wording of this section "**during the lifetime of the person who created it or within a period of fifty years following the death of that person**" will cause problems where that person is not known. The problem was solved in respect of tribal and indigenous communities by the

---

1. Doc. 18 § 90; Doc. 23 §134; Doc. 30 § 150; Doc. 39 §§ 154, 183; Doc. 48 § 169.
2. Doc. 10 § 52; Doc. 14 § 63; Doc. 18 §§ 82-86; Doc. 23 §§ 126-130; Doc. 48 § 167.
3. Doc. 48 §§ 173-177; Acts 303, 304-305.
4. Doc. 14 § 63; Doc. 18 § 83; Doc. 30 § 142; Doc. 39 §§ 146-147.
5. Doc. 18 § 82.
6. 123 L N T S 233.
7. Doc. 30 § 142; Doc. 39 § 147.
8. Doc. 30 § 142.
9. Acts 303.
10. *Export of Works of Art 1994-1995: Forty-first Report of the Reviewing Committee* (U.K.) HMSO Cm 3008 October 1995, 22-23.

special provision of Article 7(2): it remains, however, in respect of religious art, where the creator may be deliberately unidentified[11]. A draft section which would have allowed dating from the object itself was deleted at the Diplomatic Conference[12]. It is anomalous that because of this drafting a State should be unable to recuperate an article which may be of considerable importance and where the creator concerned had no interest in international marketability whatever — indeed, would have been distressed by the treatment of his or her creation as a commodity!

Article 7(2)

> Notwithstanding the provisions of sub-paragraph (b) of the preceding paragraph, the provisions of this Chapter shall apply where a cultural object was made by a member or members of a tribal or indigenous community for traditional or ritual use by that community and the object will be returned to that community.

Article 7(2) provides an exception to the exception. It was intended to cover the case of ethnographic objects where the creator may not be known. Where objects of ritual or worship are concerned which are removed from a tribal community, contrary to the wishes of that community, why should it be unable to recover? It is not always easy to prove the removal from such a community was "theft", but this is a kind of illicit trade which may have very severe repercussions not only on the cultural life, but even on the cohesion, of the society concerned[13]. Such objects are often in high demand for the illicit trade because "tribal art" raises high prices on the international market. An example is provided by the case of the Afo-a-Kom, a ritual figure of supreme importance, said to have embodied the spirit of the Kom (Cameroon)[14]. Elsewhere also, as in Asia and the Pacific area, there are important carvings in traditional style representing spirits. Ritual objects such as masks which in traditional communities (as among Native Americans) are often replaced, and the carver may even be known, but these objects are made for the community and seen as belonging to it.

A provision exempting ethnographic objects whose artist was unknown from the rule of Article 7(1)(b) was proposed at the third meeting of Governmental Experts[15]. The Australian and Canadian delegations, as also that of the United States, were particularly interested in this issue, as was UNESCO, but this complex of cultural considerations affecting indigenous and other traditional communities was not familiar to many of the delegates, and considerable discussion was necessary before the principle was accepted[16].

The effect of 7(2) now is that the provisions of Article 5 shall apply, i.e. there can be a claim for a cultural object, which was illegally exported during the lifetime of its creator or within 50 years of his or her death if the object was made by a member of an indigenous community for the use of that community.

The wording "**tribal or indigenous community**" is parallel in each of the three provisions now applying to indigenous cultural materials (Articles 3(8), 5(3)(d) and 7(2)). As to the meaning of "indigenous community," see Appendices VI and VII.

---

11. As pointed out by the Thai Delegate to the Diplomatic Conference, Acts 304.
12. Acts 304.
13. The revelation, under considerable pressure, of a hiding place of *tjuringa* which were subsequently taken, led to the death of the unfortunate informer; details given in work cited p. 24, n. 23, 883-884.
14. Nchoji Nkwi, P. "A Conservation Dilemma over African Royal Art in Cameroon" in McIntosh & Schmidt, book cited p. 48, n. 49, 98.
15. Doc. 39 §§ 144-146.
16. Doc. 48 §§ 161-165, 181; Acts 213, 215; 304-305.

ARTICLE 8

This article deals with the bodies which are competent for claims and requests.

Article 8(1)

> A claim under Chapter II and a request under Chapter III may be brought before the courts or other competent authorities of the Contracting State where the cultural object is located, in addition to the courts or other competent authorities otherwise having jurisdiction under the rules in force in Contracting States.

The debate on the phrase "**court or other competent authority**" has already been discussed in relation to Article 5 (1)[1].

A claim can be brought either in the jurisdiction where the object is located or in any other jurisdiction having competence, such as that having competence over the possessor[2]. The Secretary-General of the Hague Conference on Private International Law, a member of the Study Group, pointed out that the use of a court in the jurisdiction where the object was located was in fact a new ground of jurisdiction, being almost unknown in relation to claims for the recovery of movable property in Europe. It was considered necessary to provide this latter head of jurisdiction since an owner or requesting State may discover the whereabouts of an object in a jurisdiction bound by the Convention but not be able to bring an action against the possessor because he or she is in a jurisdiction not covered by the Convention. In the case of cultural property missing objects frequently are found when offered for sale in an auction house or by a dealer in a country with a major art trade, although the vendor is not in that jurisdiction. This is a special head of jurisdiction *in addition* to those already existing (as, for example, in the case of theft where the existing rules already provide for jurisdiction)[3]. The Irish Law Reform Commission has also pointed out that this is likely to improve enforcement, since problems of enforcement of a foreign judgment ordering return will not arise[4].

The Diplomatic Conference spent a good deal of time on this article, but, although the drafting has been improved and the substance of the article clarified, there is little modification[5].

Mis-statements about the jurisdictional rules of the Convention serve to support Lalive's view that many who pontificate on the effect of the Convention have no knowledge of the existing state of the law and therefore do not understand its effect. Consider this statement

> The law under which a claim is to be resolved is that of the country of origin, not of the country in which it is lodged.

---

1. See also Article 16.
2. Doc. 3, Art. 8; discussed Doc. 14 §§ 91-95; Doc. 18 §§ 91-93; Doc. 23 §§ 147-151.
3. Doc. 18 §§ 128-131; Doc. 23 §§ 147-150; Doc. 30 §§ 178-180; Doc. 48 § 211.
4. Consultation Paper cited p. 22, n. 6, 35.
5. Acts 224-232, 307.

> A Greek who tells an American dealer showing in Maastricht that a Goya was stolen in Italy will have the picture's future determined by an Athens Court[6].

The seriousness of the vociferous opposition of some sections of the art trade to the Convention can be evaluated by such wildly inaccurate statements.

Article 8(2)

> The parties may agree to submit the dispute to any court or other competent authority or to arbitration.

Article 8(2) provides another possibility: the use of another forum by choice between the parties, including arbitration. Some members of the Study Group considered the choice of forum to be an essential procedural freedom for the parties and that its omission might deter some States from participation in the Convention. The advantages of arbitral procedures for confidentiality have also been emphasised[7]. The provision was relatively uncontroversial[8].

Article 8 (3)

> Resort may be had to the provisional, including protective, measures available under the law of the Contracting State where the object is located even when the claim for restitution or request for return of the object is brought before the courts or other competent authorities of another Contracting State.

A clause such as Article 8(3) which provides for applications for provisional measures from a court of the state of location of the object, even if the action is brought in another jurisdiction, was proposed at the second meeting of Governmental Experts, to enable, in particular, the safeguarding of an object e.g. by prohibiting its further export during the course of legal proceedings[9] or its disappearance or destruction by inappropriate handling[10]. This is important because of the need to secure an object which is being offered for sale and to ensure that it is withdrawn, for example, from an auction. In present practice auction houses do not disclose the names of buyers. Unless there is the possibility of a court order securing the object pending the result of litigation, therefore, the object may well be lost before the claimant or requesting State has been able to get a judgment. This article was also relatively uncontroversial[11].

How exactly claims by robbed owners and requests by States are to be processed is dealt with by Article 16 (see below).

Another proposal came to the fourth meeting of experts — it would have given jurisdiction also to the court or other competent authority of the State where the theft or illegal export took place[12].

---

6. Art. cited p. 51, n. 61.
7. Doc. 14, 25; Doc. 30, 48.
8. Doc. 18 §§ 94-95, Doc. 48 §§ 211, 214; Acts 308. Other advantages of arbitration with particular reference to this Convention such as neutrality, expertise, speed, efficiency and cost have been described by Sidorsky, E. "The 1995 UNIDROIT Convention on Stolen or Illegally Exported Cultural Objects" 5 I.J.C.P. (1996) 19, 32-37.
9. Doc. 30 § 182.
10. Acts 232.
11. Doc. 30 §§ 181-183, Doc. 48 § 218, Acts 309.
12. Introduced in Doc. 29, 64 at the second meeting of Governmental Experts and discussed Doc. 30 §§ 184-186; Doc. 48 §§ 224-226.

This would have brought a complete change to the scheme of the Convention. Until then all decisions for return would have been made by the court or competent authority of another State. Since the claimant could well be the State itself where the theft took place, and certainly would be the requesting State in the case of illicit export, this would deprive a defendant of the possibility of the intervention of another authority not involved in the dispute, and was unacceptable to many States, especially those which have guarantees of private property. The proposal was defeated at the fourth meeting of the Governmental Experts, along with a proposal to include four other clauses on the enforcement of judgments. The meeting was of the opinion that enforcement should be left to the existing rules to resolve[13]. The issue was referred to at the Diplomatic Conference in the same sense[14].

---

13. Doc. 36, 43 ff.; Doc. 48 §§ 222-226.
14. Acts 248.

ARTICLE 9

This is one of the most important articles of the Convention. As we have seen, the Loewe preliminary draft presupposed that what was being prepared was a "minimum set of uniform rules" for the protection of cultural property[1]. It was understood that States which already accorded a wide measure of protection to the dispossessed owner could not be expected to reduce that protection for the sake of uniformity (especially since this would make cultural objects *less* protected than other movables - exactly the reverse of the aim of the Convention which was to give them better protection). Accordingly, from the first draft onwards, this provision appeared allowing the Parties to the future instrument to go further in the direction of protecting such persons[2]. It was also pointed out that some States accorded greater protection to both dispossessed owners and States from which cultural objects had been illegally exported, and that it was not intended to change this[3] (86 States are, at the time writing this article, party to the UNESCO Convention[4] and most States party to that Convention already give more favourable treatment).

It should be noted that a specific clause in the Preamble now states that "the provision of any remedies, such as compensation, needed to effect restitution and return in some States, does not imply that such remedies should be adopted in other States" (Preamble para. 5).

As the Secretariat report makes clear

> a consensus emerged to the effect that legal traditions were so deep-rooted that there was little prospect of achieving a solution which had escaped the authors of the draft LUAB in the sense of devising a uniform rule acceptable to all Parties to any future instrument without qualification, even if the application of that rule were to be limited to cultural objects. On the other hand it was apparent that those States which already accorded a wide measure of protection to the dispossessed owner could scarcely be expected to reduce that protection for the sake of uniformity and the idea of establishing certain conditions under which the object must be returned to the person formerly in possession while leaving it open to the Parties to the future instrument to go further in the direction protecting such persons . . . enjoyed considerable support[5].

The idea that "theft" should cover other culpable acts such as "conversion, fraud, intentional misappropriation of lost property or any other culpable act assimilated thereto" appeared in the Loewe preliminary draft[6] and would have breached the possible differences in the concept of "theft" between different systems of law - some of which would have included these other culpable acts and some of which would not[7]. It was not clear how easy it would be for States to adopt similar rules on this question, and ultimately the matter has been left to this Article to resolve.

---

1. Doc. 10 § 19; see p. 20, n. 10.
2. Doc. 3, Art. 9 discussed Doc. 14 §§ 97-100.
3. Doc. 14 § 98.
4. See Appendix V.
5. Doc. 10 §§ 17, 18.
6. Doc. 3, Art. 2.
7. See p. 31, nn. 21-22 and related text.

The view not to expressly widen theft to cover these other categories was reinforced by the decision taken at the third meeting of the Study Group to require return of a stolen cultural object in all circumstances. It was then felt that this obligation, which was wider than originally proposed in Dr. Loewe's preliminary draft, would be more difficult of acceptance if it also covered a wider group of cases than some States already included in the notion of theft[8]. Finally the view seems to have been adopted of those delegates who, at the third meeting of Governmental Experts thought that "the notion of theft, for the purpose of the Convention, was not the restrictive notion of certain national laws, but rather a broader, autonomous one which would of necessity encompass similar acts"[9].

Article 9(1)

Nothing in this Convention shall prevent a Contracting State from applying any rules more favourable to the restitution or the return of stolen or illegally exported cultural objects than provided for by this Convention.

Precisely how the preservation of and encouragement to rules more favourable to the return of cultural property was to be achieved, however, consumed much discussion. The first, Loewe, formula was a simple, one-sentence formulation[10]. It had some difficulties, however, and was redrafted many times[11]. Some experts thought it desirable to spell out the particular ways in which more favourable treatment could be given[12] and this was done, producing a much more complex formula which read:

Each Contracting State shall remain free in respect of claims brought before its courts or competent authorities:

(a) for the restitution of a stolen cultural object:

    (i)   to extend the provisions of Chapter II to acts other than theft whereby the claimant has wrongfully been deprived of possession of the object;

    (ii) to apply its national law when this would permit an extension of the period within which a claim for restitution of the object may be brought under Article 3(2);

    (iii) to apply its national law when this would disallow the possessor's right to compensation even when the possessor has exercised the necessary diligence contemplated by Article 4(1).

(b) for the return of a cultural object removed from the territory of another Contracting State contrary to the export legislation of that State:

    (i) to have regard to interests other than those material under Article 5(3);

    (ii) to apply its national law when this would permit the application of Article 5 in cases otherwise excluded by Article 7.

---

8.   Doc. 18 §§ 41-43; Doc. 39 § 60.
9.   Doc. 39 § 60. Droz, art. cited p. 22, n. 4 § 16 takes the narrower view.
10. Doc. 3, Art. 9.
11. Doc. 14 §§ 97-98; Doc. 18 §§ 132-142; Doc. 23 §§ 158-163; Doc. 30 §§ 200-207; Doc. 39 §§ 195-197; Doc. 48 §§ 243-250; Acts 232-237, 310-311.
12. Doc. 18, §§ 136-142.

(c) to apply the convention notwithstanding the fact that the theft or illegal export of the cultural object occurred before the entry into force of the Convention for that State[13].

After further discussion, the Observer from UNESCO produced a draft which tried to reflect all the additional elements which had been suggested[14]. The result was a quite complex article which produced further possible problems and achieved a degree of detail which had been avoided in other articles of the Convention, the preference in drafting being to retain simply expressed general rules to be interpreted and amplified by national legislation as necessary. The Chairman therefore asked the fourth meeting of Governmental Experts to consider whether it wanted to retain and work on the detailed draft, or to return to the more simple formula. The meeting decided to revert to the more simple formula[15].

Nonetheless, it is useful to mention what was more favourable treatment as accepted by the experts and was spelt out in the more detailed version of the article. It included

(i)   extending the provisions of Chapter II on theft to other wrongful acts such as conversion and fraud (which are included in the concept of theft in some jurisdictions but not in others)[16];

(ii)   applying the Convention notwithstanding that the date of the theft or illicit export occurred before the entry into force of the Convention[17];

(iii)   extending the period within which a claim may be brought[18];

(iv)   disallowing the possessor's claim to compensation after return of a stolen article even when he or she has used the necessary diligence (this enables Common Law countries to retain their existing law concerning the *nemo dat* rule)[19];

(v)   in the case of an illegally exported cultural object, having regard to interests of the requesting State other than those listed in Article 5(3)[20];

(vi)   disallowing the possessor's right to compensation under Article 6[21];

(vii)   applying Article 5 even in cases excluded by Article 7[22];

(viii)   disallowing the possessor the options specified in Article 6(2)[23];

(ix)   requiring that costs under Article 6(4) be met by a party other than the requesting State[24];

(x)   permitting claims outside the limitation periods set by Articles 3(3)-(8) and 5(5)[25]; and

(xi)   applying the Convention also in domestic transactions[26].

It is important to note that it is the State before whose courts the claim or request is brought which has the options; they cannot be forced upon it by the Requesting State or anyone else[27]. This article enables States to retain more favourable rules and encourages others to adopt them.

---

13. Doc. 18, Annex III.
14. Acts 104-106.
15. Doc. 48 §§ 245, 250.
16. Text quoted above from Doc 18, Annex III, Art. 11(a)(i).
17. Text quoted above, Art. 11(c).
18. Text quoted above, Art. 11(a)(ii).
19. Text quoted above, Art. 11(a)(iii).
20. Text quoted above, Art. 11(b) (i).
21. Doc. 30 §§ 203, 206.
22. Text quoted above, Art. 11(b)(ii).
23. Doc. 30 § 206.
24. Doc. 30 § 206.
25. Text quoted above Art. 11(a)(ii).
26. Doc. 23 § 42.
27. Doc. 18 §§ 140-141; Doc. 23 § 162; Acts 232-233.

Article 9(2)

> This article shall not be interpreted as creating an obligation to recognise or enforce a decision of a court or other competent authority of another Contracting State that departs from the provisions of this Convention.

This provision originated at the Diplomatic Conference with a French proposal derived from a concern that the effect of Article 9(1) would be to deprive the good faith possessor of compensation when the object was returned and might result in forum shopping. This concern was not shared by other delegations, who felt that the same result would apply even without the Convention by virtue of the differences between the legal systems on the transfer of movables (see discussion on Article 3(1)) and the rules as to enforcement of judgments. It was also pointed out that the applicable law would seldom automatically be the *lex fori*, as in most cases the applicable law would be designated by the choice of law rules according to the private international law system of the *lex fori*, the *lex causae* being that of the State of the location of the object at the time of its acquisition. It therefore seemed unnecessary to change the article[28].

The concern seemed to be based on a fear that French courts might be asked to enforce a judgment of a court in another contracting state which would require a French citizen to return a cultural object without compensation in a case where, had it been a purely domestic situation, he or she would have retained it[29]. This concern clearly ignored the view of Professor Chatelain which had been so influential in establishing the changes concerned with the *bona fide* purchaser.

At any rate, it does not appear that Article 9(2) changes the existing legal position. The Convention was never intended to produce general uniform rules; from the first meeting of the Study Group the aim was expressed to be the establishment of minimum uniform rules[30] and the retention of more favourable rules can hardly be seen as an implementation of the Convention which "**departs from the provisions of this Convention**"[31] as it was one of the fundamental conditions for its acceptance. In any event, if the applicable law were determined by a French court to be that of a country which would order return without requiring compensation, then it would have to apply it[32], just as the English court applied Italian law in *Winkworth v. Christie*[33]. Conversely, a French court applying the Convention could not in any case be required by the Convention to apply a decision of a foreign court which was not compatible with the Convention.

Article 9(2) in its present form was settled by the compromise working group and was not seen by the Drafting Committee[34]. The precise reasoning behind its wording is therefore not available.

---

28. Acts 232-237, 310.
29. Acts 232 (Sanson), 234 (Baur), 310 (Baur).
30. See p. 20, n. 10 and related text.
31. As specified in the Preamble: see discussion of Preamble, para. 5.
32. This is the preliminary view of the Irish Law Reform Commission in the Consultation Paper cited p. 22 n. 6.
33. Case cited p. 22, n. 3.
34. Acts 311.

ARTICLE 10

Few issues caused more discussion within[1], and more alarm outside[2], the expert discussions than that of retroactivity. From the first meeting of the Study Group it was clear that, although there was a substantial amount of agreement among experts and States alike that something should be done to limit illicit traffic for the future, a draft which tried to deal with past issues would have little hope of success. The statement that

> applying UNIDROIT retroactively would lead to the virtual emptying of ancient art collections in museums[3]

distorts the reality of the discussions, since such general retroactive application was never in question.

There were two views in the discussions: on the one hand, that a Convention is not as a general rule retroactive and therefore that a clause was not necessary, and on the other, that it would be wise (even if not necessary) to insert a clause on non-retroactivity to reassure those who were worried that it might be.

In favour of the first view was urged the general rule of the Vienna Convention on the Law of Treaties (Art. 28) which provides that

> Unless a different intention appears from the treaty or is established, its provisions do not bind a party in relation to any act or fact which took place or any situation which ceased to exist before the date of entry into force of the treaty with respect to that party[4].

This clause represents long-standing custom in international law. The same arguments were raised during the drafting of the 1970 UNESCO Convention. Although the insertion of a provision specifying that the Convention was not retroactive was considered during its preparation, it was found unnecessary to include it[5] and it has never been argued that it is retroactive. Indeed, an alternative procedure has been set up within UNESCO to deal with cases which do not fall within the terms of the 1970 Convention[6].

In favour of the second view it was argued that, to reassure laymen who did not necessarily understand the legal rules as to non-retroactivity, a clause should be expressly included. At the Diplomatic Conference, some Delegations stated that an express clause on non-retroactivity was essential if their States were to become party[7].

---

1. Doc. 14 §§ 102-108; Doc. 18 §§ 143-148; Doc. 23 §§ 153-158; Doc. 30 §§ 192-199; Doc. 39 §§ 192-194; Doc. 48 §§ 206-208, 229-242; Acts 249-253.
2. *Statement of Position of Concerned Members of the American Cultural Community regarding the UNIDROIT Convention on Stolen and Illegally Exported Cultural Objects* 1995, 31 May 1995, 27.
3. Ibid.
4. Cited p. 19, n. 1. Currently 81 States are party to this Convention.
5. Special Committee 1969, reported in UNESCO Doc. 16 C/17 Annex II, 6.
6. UNESCO Intergovernmental Committee for Promoting the Return of Cultural Property to its Countries of Origin or its Restitution in Case of Illicit Appropriation established in 1978. Its ninth session was held in Paris from 16-19 September 1996. For a discussion of its activities see Prott & O'Keefe, book cited p. 24, n. 23, 855-862.
7. Acts 249 (Netherlands), 249 (Germany), 252 (United Kingdom).

The Loewe preliminary draft included such a clause[8]. However this caused certain misunderstandings by other States. One representative said that it was be impossible to accept "that an illegal act may become legal simply because it was committed before the entry into force of the proposed Convention"[9] or that the Convention "should erase the past at a single stroke"[10]. It was explained that the establishment of the Convention would have no such effect, but that the inclusion of such a clause would simply exclude such cases from the particular procedures of the Convention. Nevertheless, whatever the real legal effect, the Convention could be interpreted by laymen in another sense, and for many governments of countries which had already lost their most outstanding cultural objects this was an issue which could affect the political future of the government itself.

At the fourth session of Governmental Experts, therefore, the clause was left out[11]. This became an issue seized upon by dealers and others who disliked the idea of the Convention and who then argued, wrongly, that the intention of the Convention and its drafters was to apply its terms retrospectively[12]. Certain proposals for partial retroactivity were proposed during the meetings of Governmental Experts, but none were retained[13].

This background is necessary to understand the compromise finally reached at the Diplomatic Conference.

Article 10(1)

> The provisions of Chapter II shall apply only in respect of a cultural object that is stolen after this Convention enters into force in respect of the State where the claim is brought, provided that:
>
> (a) the object was stolen from the territory of a Contracting State after the entry into force of this Convention for that State; or
>
> (b) the object is located in a Contracting State after the entry into force of the Convention for that State.

This provision was designed to deal with the temporal range of the Convention. However this article tries to take account of cases where more than two countries are concerned and in doing so has given rise to some questions of interpretation.

The alternatives considered in respect of retroactivity were summarized by the Chairman of the Committee of the Whole[14]. The text which came from the Drafting Committee did not include such a clause but it became part of the compromise text of the special working group whose discussions have not been reported[15].

---

8. Doc. 3, Art. 10.
9. Doc. 23 § 10.
10. Acts 166 (Cameroon).
11. Doc. 48 §§ 239-242.
12 . Although some States expressed their wishes in this regard at the Diplomatic Conference, this was never a serious negotiating position for the States with collections with substantial foreign collections, Acts 249-253.
13. Fraoua, art. cited p. 15, n. 1, 325.
14. Acts 252-253.
15. Acts 151.

Some delegations thought that the Convention should be applied to objects wherever stolen[16] (and hence whether or not the Convention was in force in the State of theft at the time of the theft). Such a rule would not have been adopted without precedent: The Protocol to the Convention on the Protection of Cultural Property in the Event of Armed Conflict 1954 (the "Hague Convention"), provides that Contracting Parties will take into custody cultural property imported into their territory either directly or indirectly from any occupied territory and will return the objects to the competent authorities in the occupied territory[17]. The obligation is not limited to the territory of other Parties to the Convention[18]. Other delegates to the UNIDROIT negotiations thought that the object must have been both stolen in a Contracting State and claimed in a Contracting State and that the Convention must be in force in both States at the time of theft.

If a stolen cultural object is claimed in the State of the possessor, this conforms to the normal jurisdictional rules as mentioned in Article 8(1), and Article 10(1)(a) simply makes it clear that the object has to have been stolen after the date of entry into force for both of these States. It is irrelevant whether it has entered into force for the State where the object may be located. Whether the judgment could be enforced in the State of location would depend on that State's rules as to enforcement of foreign judgments, including any treaties by which it might be bound.

If the stolen cultural object is claimed in the State of location, this is the exceptional ground of jurisdiction provided by Article 8(1) and Article 10(1) (introduction) makes it clear that the object must have been stolen after the date of entry into force of the Convention for the Contracting State of location. The judge in the State of location will have to decide according to the rules in force there by what right the claimant asserts a claim under the Convention: whether the claimant had the object stolen from him in a Contracting State after the date of entry into force of the Convention for that State or whether he is domiciled in a Contracting State or whatever connecting factor the judge adopts in that jurisdiction for such cases. But there clearly must have been a reason for adding clause (b).

Could an object be claimed under Article 10(1)(b) notwithstanding that it had been stolen in a State which is not party to the Convention at all? This could occur if an object was stolen while on temporary loan in another country. It may be that this provision was inserted to cover the case where the owner would otherwise be entitled to make a claim (i.e. he is domiciled in a contracting State which is party to the Convention at the date of theft) and wishes to sue the possessor in a country which is also a Contracting State and was at the time of the theft. This would explain the reasoning behind Article 10(1)(b), although, as we do not have a record of the discussions of the working group, it must be speculation.

On the other hand, because Article 10 deals with the temporal application of the Convention, it could be argued that the spatial field of application has not been dealt with, other than the mention of "claims of an international character" in Article 1, nor have the qualifications of claimants been set out. These would normally be established by the judge where the claim is made "under the rules in force in Contracting States" (Article 8(1)). The fact that these issues are not dealt with elsewhere might suggest, however, that this article also deals with these matters i.e. that it deals not only with the occurrence of the theft after the entry into force of the Convention for the relevant States, but also with what are the relevant States for the purpose of assessing the

---

16. Doc. 48 §§ 22-24; see also discussion in Acts 156-157.
17. Articles 3 & 4.
18. Protocol and Art. 18(3) of the Convention on the Protection of Cultural Property in the Event of Armed Conflict 1954 (the "Hague Convention"), the text of which is given in Appendix IX.

applicability of the Convention, and what link the claimant (if it is not the State itself) has with the Contracting State. Because of the mobility of cultural objects, their frequent appearance in other countries by way of loan, deposit, exhibition or transit, and the possibilities of theft in all these contexts, very complex situations may arise.

Because of the history of this article it can be argued that it should be read narrowly as applying only to the time element. In other respects judges should be left to interpret and apply the Convention. But even supposing the other view were taken, i.e. that States would apply the Convention to cultural objects even if stolen in a non-Contracting State, this view might be restricted to the case of the temporary loan, which would not be an unreasonable application of the philosophy of the Convention, and even if the broader view were taken, this should not suggest that it is unnecessary to become party to the Convention provided other States do. One cannot imagine that an owner in a non-Contracting State can expect to automatically have the advantage of suing in a Contracting State, because the judge in the jurisdiction where the object is claimed will still have to ensure that the claimant has a justification for seeking the benefit of the Convention, i.e. some kind of link (as specified in that jurisdiction) with a Contracting State.

A Contracting State, may, of course, prefer to accord more generous rules under Article 9.

Finally, it should be noted that the most important factor, as specified in the introduction of Article 10(1), is that the State where the claim is brought must have been party to the Convention at the time of the theft. This is an assurance that no claim can be brought for any object stolen before six months after the deposit of the appropriate instrument of participation. As the Convention is not yet in force, has to date three full participants and will not come into force even in those Contracting States before six months after the date of the deposit of the fifth such instrument, this means that no claim can be brought in respect of any object stolen before 1998. What the Convention does is to put purchasers on notice that **from now on** they will be responsible for return if they do not make efforts to ensure that a cultural object which they are acquiring is not stolen after that date (or whatever date will apply in that jurisdiction).

Article 10(2)

> The provisions of Chapter III shall apply only in respect of a cultural object that is illegally exported after this Convention enters into force for the requesting State as well as the State where the request is brought.

If an illegally exported cultural object is claimed in the State of the possessor, then the object has to have been illegally exported after the date of entry into force for both the State where the claim is made and for the State of illegal export. The status of the Convention in the State of location at that time does not seem to be relevant. If the claim is made in the State of location, then it does not matter whether the State where the possessor could have been sued was a party to the Convention at the date of illegal export or not, but the Convention must have been in force in the State of location and the State of illegal export at the time of illegal export.

Although a member of the Study Group had suggested that a Contracting State should, if all the necessary conditions were satisfied, also return cultural objects to a non-Contracting State whose export legislation had been violated[19] , this suggestion was not accepted and was not subsequently discussed. More generous treatment can, of course, be accorded under Article 9.

---

19. Doc. 10 § 45.

In a Canadian prosecution for illegal import of a Nigerian terra cotta head of the Nok culture under its legislation implementing the UNESCO Convention 1970, the prosecution failed because the Nigerian government did not bring evidence that the export occurred after the coming into force of export control legislation. The case is unfortunate, since it seems clear that Nigeria had required written permission for the export of antiquities since 1929 and the Nok culture was only discovered in 1943[20]. The Canadian implementing legislation was silent on the issue of when the illegal export had to take place in relation to that law and to the entry into force of the Convention. On one view, it was open to the Canadian judge to decide that the critical date was the date of import[21]. In the case of the Coroma textiles, Bolivia did prove to the satisfaction of the court that export controls had been in force at the date of export[22]. The additional requirement to prove that the illegal imports occurred after the entry into force of the UNIDROIT Convention will be an additional evidentiary problem for requesting States unless, of course, a State accords more favourable treatment under Article 9. Concern was expressed on this point during the Diplomatic Conference, but a proposal by Israel that failure to prove the date of export should give rise to a presumption that it had taken place after the date of entry into force of the Convention[23] was not adopted.

The formulation in Article 10(1) and 10(2) has been balanced, however, by assertions in other parts of the Convention, making clear that this does not imply recognition of any prior illegal transactions (Preamble § 6; Art 10(3)).

Article 10 (3)

> This Convention does not in any way legitimise any illegal transaction of whatever nature which has taken place before the entry into force of this Convention or which is excluded under paragraphs (1) or (2) of this article, nor limit any right of a State or other person to make a claim under remedies available outside the framework of this Convention for the restitution or return of a cultural object stolen or illegally exported before the entry into force of this Convention.

This paragraph was the result, again, of the working group's compromise and provides that the UNIDROIT Convention does not legitimate any prior illegal transaction, nor restrict a State from claiming back such items, in private law, by bilateral negotiation, inter-institutional arrangements or through the UNESCO Committee mentioned above.

---

20. *R. v. Heller* (1983) 27 Alta. L.R. (2d) 346; (1984) 51 A.R. 73 (Q.B.) [Canada]. See discussion of this case in Prott & O'Keefe, book cited p. 24, n. 23, 778-779.
21. Id. 778-780.
22. Case cited p. 58, n. 35.
23. Acts 250 (Vrellis), 251 (Lazaru, Francioni), 252 (Yifhar).

FINAL CLAUSES

The final clauses of the Convention were based on usual UNIDROIT practice and most do not call for comment. One or two should, however, be mentioned.

Article 13

(1) This Convention does not affect any international instrument by which any Contracting State is legally bound and which contains provisions on matters governed by this Convention, unless a contrary declaration is made by the States bound by such instrument.

(2) Any Contracting State may enter into agreements with one or more Contracting States, with a view to improving the application of this Convention in their mutual relations. The States which have concluded such an agreement shall transmit a copy to the depositary.

This provision allows the survival of any earlier Convention dealing with the same subject matter unless the States bound by that instrument make a declaration to the contrary (Art. 13(1))[1]. Such an article had already been proposed during the working sessions of the Governmental Experts[2], but it was decided to leave discussion to the Diplomatic Conference where it was dealt with among the final clauses[3], States may also enter new agreements on the same subject matter which will improve the application of the Convention in their mutual relations (Article 13(2)). This may include, for example, spelling out the more favourable terms which will be accorded reciprocally to each other according to the facility provided in Article 9 to give more favourable treatment to the return of cultural property than is provided in the Convention.

Finally, States which are Members of regional bodies or "organisations of economic integration" may declare that they will apply the internal rules of these bodies as between themselves. At the ceremony for the signing of the Final Act of the Diplomatic Conference, France made such a declaration on behalf of the members of the European Union. It should be noted that the 53 States of the English-speaking Commonwealth have adopted a scheme, to be based on model legislation, between themselves concerning illicit export (theft is already considered adequately dealt with by the Common Law, although the more generous limitation periods in the UNIDROIT Convention may prove to be attractive) (Appendix VIII).

Article 16

(1) Each Contracting State shall at the time of signature, ratification, acceptance, approval or accession, declare that claims for the restitution, or requests for the return, of cultural objects brought by a State under Article 8 may be submitted to it under one or more of the following procedures:

---

1. Originally proposed by the Israeli Delegation, Doc. 30 § 208.
2. Doc. 48 §§ 251-252.
3. Acts 339 (Art. D).

(a) directly to the courts or other competent authorities of the declaring State;

(b) through an authority or authorities designated by that State to receive such claims or requests and to forward them to the courts or other competent authorities of that State;

(c) through diplomatic or consular channels.

(2) Each Contracting State may also designate the courts or other authorities competent to order the restitution or return of cultural objects under the provisions of Chapters II and III.

(3) Declarations made under paragraphs 1 and 2 of this article may be modified at any time by a new declaration.

(4) The provisions of paragraphs 1 to 3 of this article do not affect bilateral or multilateral agreements on judicial assistance in respect of civil and commercial matters that may exist between Contracting States.

This clause had not been considered at any of the experts' meetings[4], and the report of the Final Clauses Committee[5] records no discussion on it. Nonetheless it is of some importance and Article 16(1)(b) reflects the institution of the system of central authorities established by the Commonwealth Scheme (Art. 6) and European Directive (Art. 4). Efforts at previous meetings to insert the mechanism of central authorities had not been successful[6]. It is therefore doubly unfortunate that there was no discussion of the clause as approved at the Diplomatic Conference.

If, for example, a State requesting return of an illegally exported cultural object is to apply directly to a court in the requested State, the requested State will have to ensure that a procedure, which may not previously have existed, is in place for such requests. If this is a completely novel claim, then even experienced lawyers in the jurisdiction concerned will need orientation before the system can be seen to be working adequately. On the other hand, existing procedures may be sufficient: in the case of the illegally exported Taranaki panels, the New Zealand government was able to argue right to the House of Lords before losing the case on a technical ground[7].

If either of the other procedures is to be used (lodgement with a designated authority or through diplomatic channels), it is difficult to see whether there will be a prescribed form of claim or request. Provided only that the requirements of the Convention are met, and the documents provided in a language that the relevant court or authority understands, the requested State probably has no right to insist on a particular form of claim or request. Of course, in many States implementing legislation will make the appropriate procedure clear. Experience will determine how these questions come to be regulated. States which have established a procedure of lodgement through a central authority for the purposes of another instrument such as the European Directive (Appendix XI Art. 3) or under the Commonwealth Scheme (Appendix VIII Art. 6) may decide to employ that same procedure for claims and requests under the UNIDROIT Convention.

---

4. Doc. 30 §§ 92-85; Doc. 39 §§ 89-90.
5. Acts 338-340 (Art. H).
6. Doc. 30 §§ 92-85; Doc. 39 §§ 89-90.
7. Case cited p. 32, n. 33.

Of the three States party to date, China has declared for direct access through its courts or through the competent administrative authorities for transmission to the courts, Lithuania for the central authority system (Ministry of Culture to forward to the courts) and Paraguay for diplomatic or consular channels.

Articles 17 and 20

Article 17

> Each Contracting State shall, no later than six months following the date of deposit of its instrument of ratification, acceptance, approval or accession, provide the depositary with written information in one of the official languages of the Convention concerning the legislation regulating the export of its cultural objects. This information shall be updated from time to time as appropriate.

Article 20

> The President of the International Institute for the Unification of Private Law (Unidroit) may at regular intervals, or at any time at the request of five Contracting States, convene a special committee in order to review the practical operation of this Convention.

These articles show that the negotiating States intended UNIDROIT to follow an active role in assuring the functioning of the Convention. Contracting States are to lodge information in French or English of their legislation regulating the export of cultural heritage (Art. 17) and the President of UNIDROIT may convene a special Committee to review the practical operation of the Convention. Although UNIDROIT, prior to the adoption of this Convention, had no specific experience with cultural property, its close association with UNESCO over the many years required for the adoption of this Convention has ensured a good working partnership on the relevant issues, and there is no doubt that this will continue.

Article 18

> No reservations are permitted except those expressly authorised in this Convention.

This clause provides for no reservations to the Convention "**except those expressly authorised in this Convention**". Since none are so authorised, one might wonder at the point of including the final phrase. The explanation is simple. The clause was proposed by the UNIDROIT Secretariat. In the final stressful hours of adoption of the working group's compromise text, no time was available to the drafting Committee to tidy up any remaining anomalies, and, as the clause has no substantive effect, it is probably unimportant, though inelegant.

---

8.   Acts 311.
9.   Acts 312.

The question of reservations or, in the terminology proposed by the United States Delegation, "opting out" of one of the Chapters of the Convention, was a difficult one. As has been pointed out before, the delicate balancing of many interests meant that, as in many other international negotiations, a power to make reservations could do away with the compromise achieved. This danger was more than apparent in the final session of the conference, where the United States Delegation proposed that States be given power to "opt out" of the whole of Chapter III (on illicit export)[8]. Japan then proposed that States be given the right to opt out of either Chapter II or Chapter III[9]. This clearly would have made nonsense of thirteen years work to achieve minimal uniform standards for the treatment of cultural objects, leaving nothing but the Preamble, definitions and final clauses as a possible common core. It was rejected by the Diplomatic Conference, along with the possibility of making reservations[10].

It should be noted, too, that the Convention is an integrated whole, the acceptance of many individual provisions depending on correlative provisions in other parts of the document. Thus for some the decision taken on the type of definition was critical for the acceptance of Article 3(1); the breadth of the definition relevant for the length of the limitation period; the bringing of a claim related to the suitability of the tribunal to hear it; the decision on cumulative or alternative points of departure for the running of limitations periods associated with the length of those periods[11]; the provision for compensation under Article 4(1) only acceptable for some countries with the provision of an article allowing them to keep rules more favourable to the return of the cultural object as embodied now in Article 9. This complex web of related provisions each one of which was in some way essential for some countries (as well as for the coherence of the Convention as a whole) shows how difficult it would have been to allow reservations which would have disturbed this whole carefully negotiated structure.

Other provisions

In the course of the negotiations various other provisions were proposed and discarded. Some of these were of importance — particularly those on private international law issues such as enforcement of judgments and refusal to enforce on grounds of public policy — an echo of which revived, surprisingly, after exhaustive discussions in earlier meetings, at the Diplomatic Conference and found its way into Article 9(2). The discussion on many of these proposals warrants attention, but another study would be necessary to do justice to them and to avoid unduly lengthening this one.

---

10. Acts 311-313, 354-355.
11. Doc. 48 §§ 52-60.

CONCLUSION

The UNIDROIT Convention on Stolen and Illegally Exported Cultural Objects 1995 is a major international instrument and has a real possibility of deterring illicit trade. It may be doubted whether it is going to lead to a major increase in actions for the return of cultural property - not one case has arisen under the European Directive which has now been in force three years and covers some countries suffering most actively from illicit traffic. Its impact is more likely to be on the practice of collectors and other acquirers in making them more careful in inquiring into the origins of cultural objects offered for sale.

The Convention has not achieved uniform law, but it has achieved minimum uniform rules. The experience in recent years has been that national courts increasingly seek to harmonise their interpretation of key concepts in accordance with the aims and purposes of an international treaty[1]. This is increasingly evident in the case-law collected by UNIDROIT on other harmonising Conventions.

Governments of course will need to consider its provisions very carefully. The Convention has achieved its effects with as little interference with the legal art trade as is possible if any headway is to be made against the transfer of illegally trafficked cultural objects into the licit trade. In view of the different interests involved, the different solutions in national law to the problems of illegally traded movables as well as the different considerations between theft and illegal export, the achievement of the Convention is remarkable. It now warrants serious scholarly study.

In a recent Swiss case where France sought judicial assistance for the return of a painting, the Federal Court of Public Law noted the public international interest in the return of stolen cultural property and, citing the UNESCO Convention of 1970 to which France is a party and the UNIDROIT Convention, which France, Italy and Switzerland have all signed, stated that these represent a common inspiration and thus constitute the expression of international public order either in force or in formation. It further noted the basis of the UNIDROIT Convention in Swiss law and practice and that the Convention realised an effective international weapon against illicit traffic while ensuring sufficient procedural guarantees for safeguarding the legitimate interests of the *bona fide* possessor[2].

Unfortunately some elements of the art trade have made emotional responses which are not only one-sided but often inaccurate as to the effect and purpose of the Convention. Some have already been mentioned above[3]. But what is one to make of the following statement?

> . . . a dealer at a fair in any UNIDROIT country could be bankrupted by accusations from any visitor claiming that the dealer is handling stolen goods. Under UNIDROIT regulations, such accusations can lead swiftly to confiscation of paintings and objects to an unlimited value, as well as legal action in which the accused will get no compensation for costs, even if his innocence is proved[4].

---

1. Explanatory Report § 38.
2. Case cited p. 50, n. 56.
3. Seearguments quoted at p. 19, n. 6; p. 51, n. 61; p. 72, n. 6.
4. Lemmens L.A., Secretary-General of TEFAF, reported in XXI *ARTnewsletter* No. 15, 19 March 1996, 2. A careful reading and proper understanding of Arts. 3 and 4 should make the exaggeration of such a claim evident.

Or a statement by Baroness Trumpingdon in the House of Lords, which says that UNIDROIT (whose full name is given inaccurately) "was founded by Mussolini"[5]? (UNIDROIT was founded in 1926 as a League of Nations institution and has been responsible for more than 70 studies on unification of law, more than 40 of which have resulted in international conventions. Its Secretary-General 1984 -1997 was British[6].)

Other reactions are equally exaggerated: Feilchenweldt calls the Convention "pernicious"[7] and Fitzpatrick argues that dealers, collectors and museums will find themselves constantly in court in "expensive", "time-consuming, distracting and debilitating litigation"[8], although not one claim has been made in the three years since the European Directive was adopted and it applies to a number of countries with major problems of illicit traffic and others with major markets.

Blaisot makes the following incorrect statements about the Convention: that any stolen or illegally exported cultural object whatever gives an immediate right to a request for restitution: that each State has the right to set whatever limitation periods it wishes; that if a possessor cannot present formal proof that he acquired the object before the entry into force of the Convention, restitution will follow with no appeal possible; that a possessor could be accused of receiving stolen goods and that the art market would therefore be suffocated[9].

And the collector George Ortiz claims that the UNIDROIT Convention is based on "the national patrimony claim" which "leads to retrograde ethnocentrism", and ultimately "to cultural genocide and then to physical genocide"[10]!

Small wonder that Pierre Lalive, a member of the Study Group, Chairman of the four meetings of Governmental Experts and of the Committee of the Whole at the Diplomatic Conference, speaks of the excessive, even absurd, criticisms of the Convention, issue of an ignorance of the existing law and a sort of "collective autointoxication"[11].

TEFAF (The European Fine Arts Foundation) has threatened to move the Fine Arts Fairs from Basel and Maastricht if the Swiss and Netherlands governments proceed with the ratification of the Convention[12]. (It may be difficult for them to find another home: France, Greece, Italy, Portugal, Spain and the United States are already party to the UNESCO Convention of 1970, and, following a revelation of handling of stolen and smuggled cultural property in Italy and London by employees of Sotheby's, amid calls for accession to the UNESCO Convention, the United Kingdom Department of Trade and Industry announced that it would conduct an investigation into the art trade in London[13]. The directors of the State museums of Berlin and Prussian cultural property have urged responsible Ministers in Germany to undertake appropriate action to adopt the Convention as soon as possible[14]).

---

5. House of Lords, 23 April 1996.
6 . Malcolm Evans, prematurely deceased on 23 February 1997. A special tribute is due to his patience, drive and intelligent direction of the work which resulted in the Convention.
7. Cited p. 51, n. 61.
8. Art. cited p. 27, n. 10 above.
9. Blaisot, C. "Alerte sur UNIDROIT!" 26 *Le Journal des Arts* June 1996, 52.
10. *The Art Newspaper* February 1997, 21.
11. Lalive, P., art. cited p.13, n. 7, 57. See his detailed discussion of the "anti-UNIDROIT" campaign in Switzerland and the distortions of the Convention which he there describes as well as his article cited p. 32, n. 28.
12. "Maastricht vs. Unidroit" *ARTnewsletter* 19 March 1996, 1.
13. Book cited p. 65, n. 24; *The Times* Editorial 7 February. A television documentary based on the same book also had a significant public reaction. The government spokesman later announced that Codes of Practice were believed to be sufficient.
14. Decision of 27 November 1996 (Protokoll der Direktorenkonferenz Nr. 8/96).

No one knows exactly the extent of the illicit trade. We do know that there has been a huge increase in theft of cultural objects over the last three decades[15]. Between 30,000 and 40,000 cultural objects are stolen *each year* in Italy and a similar number in France. During 1995 insurance companies paid close to $1 billion for artworks stolen in Britain alone[16]. The value of bronze and terracotta figures stolen from a single museum at Ife, in Nigeria, has been calculated at $ 250 million[17]. Customs officials in Hongkong seized $ 5.5 million worth of smuggled artefacts from China between January and July 1994[18]. A 26 minute video circulating in London in 1996 showed 24 religious paintings from Croatia for sale, each worth up to $20,000[19]. Half a million DM was the price asked for 15 paintings stolen from Czech collections which were seized by police in Germany in 1996[20]. $ 100 million is the estimate for 89 rare manuscripts stolen from the Russian National Library in 1996[21]. The number of illicitly traded objects which turn up in the hands of collectors, many of whom have bought from dealers and auctioneers whom they relied on, must be of the deepest concern for all who care about the preservation of the cultural heritage for all humanity.

States should not be deterred from the most serious efforts to apply the best international legal means to deter that illicit trade.

---

15. The sobering facts are set out by Lalive, art. cited p. 32, n. 28, 15-21.
16. *The New York Times* 20 November 1995, C12.
17. Kiehlo, R. Quoted in Conway, I., "Art dealers plunder Africa of its Past" *The European* 14-20 September 1995, 5.
18. Seibert, S. et al. "Art Pirates" *Newsweek* (New York) 22 August 1994, 39.
19. Grey, S. "Bosnian art plunder sold in Britain" *The Sunday Times* 16 June 1996, 1.7.
20. Bailey, M. "Major crime ring broken" *The Art Newspaper* September 1996, 1.
21. "Special Report: Art Theft in Eastern Europe" *Art and Auction* April 1996, 20.

SELECT BIBLIOGRAPHY

(This List does not include articles written on the various drafts of the Convention, except where they have been referred to in the body of the text)

Crewdson, R. "On the Making of Conventions" 21 *International Legal Practitioner* (1996) 89-92

Droz, G. "Convention d'UNIDROIT sur les biens volés ou illicitement exportés" forthcoming in *Revue critique de droit international privé* (July 1997)

Fraoua, R. "Le projet de convention de l'UNIDROIT sur le retour international des biens culturels volés ou illicitement exportés" *Aktuelle Juristische Praxis 3/19954* 317 at 323

Hughes, V. "The UNIDROIT Convention on Stolen and Illegally Exported Cultural Objects" publd. in Canadian Museums Association Proceedings of Legal Affairs and Management Symposium (Ottawa, 1996)

Jenkins, P. "The UNIDROIT Convention on Stolen and Illegally Exported Cultural Objects" 1 *Art Antiquity and Law* (1996) 163

Lalive, P. "Une Avancée du Droit international: la Convention de Rome d'UNIDROIT sur les Biens culturels volés ou illicitement exportés" 1 *Uniform Law Review* (1996) 40-58

———————— "La Convention d'UNIDROIT sur les Biens culturels volés ou illicitement exportés (du 24 juin 1995) 1997 *Revue suisse de droit international et de droit européen* 13

Marques dos Santos, A. "Projecto de Convençao do UNIDROIT sobre a restituição internacional dos Bens culturals roubados ou ilicitamente exportados" 1996 *Direito do Patrimonio Cultural* 61

Merryman, J.H. "The UNIDROIT Convention: Three Significant Departures from the *Urtext*" 5 *International Journal of Cultural Property* (1996) 11

Prott, L.V. "Kulturgüterschutz nach der UNIDROIT Konvention und nach der UNESCO Konvention" (Protection of Cultural Property according to the UNIDROIT and UNESCO Conventions) (text in English) 95 *ZVglRWiss* (1996) 188

———————— "UNESCO and UNIDROIT: a Partnership against Illicit Trafficking" 1 *Uniform Law Review* (1996) 59-71

Reichelt, G. "Die Rolle von UNIDROIT für den Internationalen Kulturgüterschutz" in *Europa im Aufbruch: Festschrift Fritz Schwind* (1993) 205

Sidorsky, E. "The 1995 UNIDROIT Convention on Stolen or Illegally Exported Cultural Objects: The Role of International Arbitration" 5 *International Journal of Cultural Property* (1996) 19

APPENDIX I

LIST OF UNIDROIT DOCUMENTS REFERRED TO IN THE TEXT AND FOOTNOTES

All the documents relating to the UNIDROIT Convention on Stolen and Illegally Exported Cultural Objects 1995 are given the generic UNIDROIT reference "Study LXX" before the Document No.

Doc. 3 Preliminary draft Convention on the Restitution of Cultural Property drawn up by Roland Loewe (attached as Appendix II)

Doc. 10 Summary report on the first session of the Unidroit study group on the international protection of cultural property, 12-15 December 1988

Doc. 13 Notes on the first session of the UNIDROIT Study group on the international protection of cultural property by Lyndel V. Prott, March 1989

Doc. 14 Summary report on the second session of the Unidroit study group on the international protection of cultural property, 13-17 April 1989

Doc. 18 Summary report on the third session of the Unidroit study group on the international protection of cultural property, 22-26 January 1990

Doc. 23 Committee of Governmental Experts on the international protection of cultural property, Report on the first session, 6-10 May 1991

Doc. 29 Committee of Governmental Experts on the international protection of cultural property, Working Papers submitted during the second session of the committee, 20-29 January 1992

Doc. 30 Committee of Governmental Experts on the international protection of cultural property, Report on the second session, 20-29 January 1992

Doc. 38 Committee of Governmental Experts on the international protection of cultural property, Working Papers submitted during the third session of the committee, 22-26 February 1993

Doc. 39 Committee of Governmental Experts on the international protection of cultural property, Report on the third session, 22-26 February 1993

Doc. 40 Preliminary draft convention on stolen or illegally exported cultural objects

Doc. 48 Committee of Governmental Experts on the international protection of cultural property, Report on the fourth session, 29 September-8 October 1993

Explanatory Report of the UNIDROIT Secretariat accompanying the Draft UNIDROIT Convention on the International Return of Stolen and Illegally Exported Cultural Objects 1995, published in

Acts 18-42. (At the time of writing, the Explanatory Report on the final text of the Convention adopted at the Diplomatic Conference was not available.)

Acts and Proceedings of the Diplomatic Conference for the Adoption of the Draft UNIDROIT Convention on the International Return of Stolen or Illegally Exported Cultural Objects, Rome, 7-24 June 1995

APPENDIX II

PRELIMINARY DRAFT CONVENTION ON THE RESTITUTION
OF
CULTURAL PROPERTY

DRAWN UP BY MR ROLAND LOEWE

Article 1

(1)   For the purposes of this Convention, "cultural property" means any material object created by man of artistic, historical or cultural importance.

(2)   This Convention governs neither:

(a)   the question of ownership of cultural property or that of other rights which may exist over it; however, a possessor who has been obliged to make restitution of cultural property to a person who has been deprived of possession or who, in conformity with Article 4 (1), has returned it against payment of compensation to the State of origin may no longer assert ownership or any other real right thereover; nor

(b)   the liability of experts, auctioneers or other sellers of cultural property.

Article 2

(1)   When a person has been dispossessed of cultural property by theft, conversion, fraud, intentional misappropriation of lost property or any other culpable act assimilated thereto by a court acting under article 8, the possessor of such property shall make restitution of it to the dispossessed person when:

(a)   that property has, at the place where it is located, a value in excess of [100,000 Special Drawing Rights] [200,000 Swiss francs] and when the possessor fails to prove that he has consulted an expert who, before the acquisition of the property, had advised him in writing that there were no grounds to suspect that the property had been the subject of any of the culpable acts mentioned above: that expert shall be empowered to act by the authorities of a state party to this convention and his services shall be employed neither by the purchaser of the property nor by the person from whom the property may be acquired, nor yet again on the basis of any lasting professional or private relationship with the one or the other;

(b)   that property has, at the place where it is located, a value in excess of [10,000 Special Drawing Rights] [20,000 Swiss francs] and when the possessor fails to prove that he acquired it at a public auction in respect of which at least 500 catalogues or lists describing the items on sale were circulated to named persons or that he acquired it from a dealer in property of the same kind who had advised him in writing that there were no grounds to suspect that the property had been the subject of any of the culpable acts mentioned above;

(c)   that property has, at the place where it is located, a value not in excess of [10,000 Special Drawing Rights] [20,000 Swiss francs] and when the possessor fails to prove that, at the time of its acquisition, he acted with the caution to be expected of an honest purchaser aware of the fact that many items of cultural property are removed from those formerly in possession of them by culpable acts.

(2)   The conduct of a predecessor in possession from whom the possessor has acquired the property by inheritance or otherwise gratuitously shall be imputed to the possessor.

(3)   When the cultural property in question has, at the time of the culpable act mentioned in paragraph (1), been located in a place open to the public such as a museum, an exhibition, a library, a place of religious worship or an archaeological site, the amounts of [100,000 and 10,000 Special Drawing Rights] [200,000 and 20,000 Swiss francs] shall be replaced respectively by those of [50,000 and 5,000 Special Drawing Rights] [100,000 and 10,000 Swiss francs] .

(4)   The preceding provisions of this article shall only apply if the action for restitution is brought before a court:

(a)   in respect of property mentioned under paragraph 1(a) within thirty years of the dispossession;

(b)   in respect of property mentioned under paragraphs 1 (b) and (c) within ten years of the dispossession.

Article 3

(1)   Any dispossessed person who is entitled to the return of cultural property shall at the same time, but at his own option, compensate the possessor either for the price paid by the latter or by his predecessor under article 2 (2) or for a sum corresponding to the actual value of the property at the place where it is located.

(2)   Paragraph (1) of this article shall not apply and no compensation shall be due when the dispossessed person proves that the possessor or his predecessor under article 2 (2) acquired the property with knowledge that it had been the subject of a culpable act or in circumstances in which a reasonable purchaser should at least have had doubts in this regard.

Article 4

(1)   When cultural property which, at the place where it is currently located, has a value in excess of [25,000 Special Drawing Rights] [50,000 Swiss francs] has, in spite of a prohibition,

been exported from the contracting State in which it was created, the state whose prohibition has been violated may request the court acting under Article 8 to order the return of the property to that state, on condition that the latter proves that the actual possessor or his predecessor under Article 2(2) had knowledge, when exporting or acquiring the property, of the export prohibition or that a reasonable person should at such time at least have had doubts in that regard.

(2)   Paragraph (1) of this article shall not apply:

(a)   when the property manifestly has a closer link with the art, history or culture of a state other than that on whose territory it was created;

(b)   when the property has been exported by a person who himself, or whose predecessor under Article 2 (2), created it or possessed it for a period of at least five years prior to its export;

(c)   when ten years have elapsed as from the time of the violation of the export prohibition.

Article 5

Any possessor required to return cultural property under Article 4 (1) may, at his option, require that the requesting State pay him a sum corresponding to the amount which would be due by a dispossessed person in conformity with article 3 (1), or transfer the property, for reward or gratuitously, to a person of his choice in the requesting State. In the latter case, the requesting State shall undertake neither to confiscate the property nor to interfere in any other way with the possession of the person to whom the property has been transferred or of his successors under a universal or individual inheritance.

[Article 6

(1)   The special drawing rights referred to in the preceding articles are those defined by the International Monetary Fund. Such rights shall be converted into the national currency of the State of the court with jurisdiction under article 8 in accordance with the value of that currency on the date on which the court is seized of the case and in accordance with the method of valuation applied by the fund for its operations and transactions.

(2)   The value of the national currency, in terms of Special Drawing Rights, of a State which is not a member of the Fund shall be calculated in a manner determined by that State.]

Article 7

(1)   In determining the value of cultural property, regard shall be had to the price applied in respect of comparable property at the place where the property is located, and in particular to the price fetched at auction sales.

(2)   For the application of Articles 2(1) and 4(1), cultural property forming part of a collection, set or series or which comes from the same collection, set or series shall be considered to be a single item of property when the same person has been deprived of possession of it or when its export has violated a prohibition, and when it is in the possession of a single person.

Article 8

The courts either of the State where the person in possession of the cultural property has his habitual residence or those of the State where the cultural property is located shall, at the option of the claimant, have jurisdiction over claims governed by this Convention. The parties to the dispute may however agree upon another jurisdiction or submit the dispute to arbitration.

Article 9

Any State Party to this Convention may extend the protection of cultural property beyond that contemplated therein, either by broadening the notion of cultural property, or by making provision for its restitution in circumstances in which such restitution is not required by the Convention by disallowing or restricting the right to compensation of the person in possession or in any other manner.

Article 10

This Convention shall apply only in respect of cultural property of which a person has been dispossessed by a culpable act or in violation of an export prohibition after the entry into force of the Convention.

APPENDIX III

PRELIMINARY DRAFT UNIDROIT CONVENTION ON STOLEN OR ILLEGALLY EXPORTED CULTURAL OBJECTS

(approved by the Unidroit study group on the international protection of cultural property at its third session on 26 January 1990)

CHAPTER I — SCOPE OF APPLICATION AND DEFINITION

Article 1

This convention applies to claims for the restitution of stolen cultural objects and for the return of cultural objects removed from the territory of a contracting state contrary to its export legislation.

Article 2

For the purpose of this convention, "cultural object" means any material object of artistic, historical, spiritual, ritual or other cultural significance.

CHAPTER II — RESTITUTION OF STOLEN CULTURAL OBJECTS

Article 3

(1)   The possessor of a cultural object which has been stolen shall return it.

(2)   Any claim for the restitution of a stolen cultural object shall be brought within a period of three years from the time when the claimant knew or ought reasonably to have known the location, or the identity of the possessor, of the object, and in any case within a period of thirty years from the time of the theft.

Article 4

(1)   The possessor of a stolen cultural object who is required to return it shall be entitled to payment at the time of restitution of fair and reasonable compensation by the claimant provided that the possessor prove that it exercised the necessary diligence when acquiring the object.

(2)   In determining whether the possessor exercised such diligence, regard shall be had to the relevant circumstances of the acquisition, including the character of the parties and the price paid, and whether the possessor consulted any accessible register of stolen cultural objects which it could reasonably have consulted.

(3)   The conduct of a predecessor from whom the possessor has acquired the cultural object by inheritance or otherwise gratuitously shall be imputed to the possessor.

CHAPTER III — RETURN OF ILLEGALLY EXPORTED CULTURAL OBJECTS

Article 5

(1)   When a cultural object has been removed from the territory of a contracting State (the requesting State) contrary to its export legislation, that State may request the court or other competent authority of a State acting under article 9 (the state addressed) to order the return of the object to the requesting State.

(2)   To be admissible, any request made under the preceding paragraph shall contain, or be accompanied by, the particulars necessary to enable the competent authority of the state addressed to evaluate whether the conditions laid down in paragraph (3) are fulfilled and shall contain all material information regarding the conservation, security and accessibility of the cultural object after it has been returned to the requesting State.

(3)   The court or other competent authority of the State addressed shall order the return of the cultural object to the requesting State if that State proves that the removal of the object from its territory significantly impairs one or more of the following interests:

(a)   the physical preservation of the object or of its context,

(b)   the integrity of a complex object,

(c)   the preservation of information of, for example, a scientific or historical character,

(d)   the use of the object by a living culture,

(e)   the outstanding cultural importance of the object for the requesting State.

Article 6

When a State has established its claim for the return of a cultural object under Article 5 (3) the court or competent authority may only refuse to order the return of that object when it finds that it has as close a, or a closer, connection with the culture of the State addressed or of a State other than the requesting State.

Article 7

The provisions of Article 5 shall not apply when:

(a)   the cultural object was exported during the lifetime of the person who created it or within a period of fifty years following the death of that person; or

(b)   no claim for the return of the object has been brought before a court or other competent authority acting under Article 9 within a period of five years from the time when the requesting State knew or ought reasonably to have known the location, or the identity of the possessor, of the object, and in any case within a period of twenty years from the date of the export of the object, or

(c)   the export of the object in question is no longer illegal at the time at which the return is requested.

Article 8

(1)   When returning the cultural object the possessor may require that, at the same time, the requesting State pay it fair and reasonable compensation unless the possessor knew or ought to have known at the time of acquisition that the object would be, or had been, exported contrary to the export legislation of the requesting State.

(2)   When returning the cultural object the possessor may, instead of requiring compensation, decide to retain ownership and possession or to transfer the object against payment or gratuitously to a person of its choice residing in the requesting State and who provides the necessary guarantees. In such cases the object shall neither be confiscated nor subjected to other measures to the same effect.

(3)   The cost of returning the cultural object in accordance with this article shall be borne by the requesting State.

(4)   The conduct of a predecessor from whom the possessor has acquired the cultural object by inheritance or otherwise gratuitously shall be imputed to the possessor.

CHAPTER IV — CLAIMS AND ACTIONS

Article 9

(1)   The claimant may bring an action under this Convention before the courts or other competent authorities of the State where the possessor of the cultural object has its habitual residence or those of the State where that object is located at the time a claim is made.

(2)   However the parties may agree to submit the dispute to another jurisdiction or to arbitration.

CHAPTER V — FINAL PROVISIONS

Article 10

This Convention shall apply only when a cultural object has been stolen, or removed from the territory of a Contracting State contrary to its export legislation, after the entry into force of the Convention in respect of the Contracting State before the courts or other competent authorities of which a claim is brought for the restitution or return of such an object.

Article 11

Each Contracting State shall remain free in respect of claims brought before its courts or competent authorities:

(a) for the restitution of a stolen cultural object:

  (i) to extend the provisions of Chapter II to acts other than theft whereby the claimant has wrongfully been deprived of possession of the object;

  (ii) to apply its national law when this would permit an extension of the period within which a claim for restitution of the object may be brought under Article 3 (2);

  (iii) to apply its national law when this would disallow the possessor's right to compensation even when the possessor has exercised the necessary diligence contemplated by Article 4 (1).

(b) for the return of a cultural object removed from the territory of another Contracting State contrary to the export legislation of that State:

  (i) to have regard to interests other than those material under Article 5 (3);

  (ii) to apply its national law when this would permit the application of Article 5 in cases otherwise excluded by Article 7.

(c) to apply the convention notwithstanding the fact that the theft or illegal export of the cultural object occurred before the entry into force of the Convention for that State.

APPENDIX IV

DIPLOMATIC CONFERENCE FOR THE ADOPTION OF THE DRAFT UNIDROIT CONVENTION ON THE INTERNATIONAL RETURN OF STOLEN OR ILLEGALLY EXPORTED CULTURAL OBJECTS

Rome, 7 to 24 June 1995

DRAFT UNIDROIT CONVENTION ON THE INTERNATIONAL RETURN OF STOLEN OR ILLEGALLY EXPORTED CULTURAL OBJECTS
(as approved by the Unidroit Committee of Governmental Experts on the international protection of cultural property on 8 October 1993)

CHAPTER I — SCOPE OF APPLICATION AND DEFINITION

Article 1

This Convention applies to claims of an international character for

(a)   the restitution of stolen cultural objects removed from the territory of a Contracting State;

(b)   the return of cultural objects removed from the territory of a Contracting State contrary to its law regulating the export of cultural objects because of their cultural significance.

Article 2

For the purposes of this Convention, cultural objects are those which, on religious or secular grounds, are of importance for archaeology, prehistory, history, literature, art or science such as those objects belonging to the categories listed in Article 1 of the 1970 UNESCO Convention on the Means of Prohibiting and Preventing the Illicit Import, Export and Transfer of Ownership of Cultural Property.

CHAPTER II — RESTITUTION OF STOLEN CULTURAL OBJECTS

Article 3

(1)   The possessor of a cultural object which has been stolen shall return it.

(2)   For the purposes of this Convention, an object which has been unlawfully excavated or lawfully excavated and unlawfully retained shall be deemed to have been stolen.

(3)   Any claim for restitution shall be brought within a period of [one] [three] year[s] from the time when the claimant knew or ought reasonably to have known the location of the object and the identity of its possessor, and in any case within a period of [thirty] [fifty] years from the time of the theft.

(4)   However, a claim for restitution of an object belonging to a public collection of a Contracting State [shall not be subject to prescription] [shall be brought within a time limit of [75] years].

[For the purposes of this paragraph, a "public collection" consists of a collection of inventoried cultural objects, which is accessible to the public on a [substantial and] regular basis, and is the property of

(i)   a Contracting State [or local or regional authority],

(ii)   an institution substantially financed by a Contracting State [or local or regional authority],

(iii)   a non profit institution which is recognised by a Contracting State [or local or regional authority] (for example by way of tax exemption) as being of [national] [public] [particular] importance, or

(iv)   a religious institution.]

Article 4

(1)   The possessor of a stolen cultural object who is required to return it shall be entitled at the time of restitution to payment by the claimant of fair and reasonable compensation provided that the possessor neither knew nor ought reasonably to have known that the object was stolen and can prove that it exercised due diligence when acquiring the object.

(2)   In determining whether the possessor exercised due diligence, regard shall be had to the circumstances of the acquisition, including the character of the parties, the price paid, whether the possessor consulted any reasonably accessible register of stolen cultural objects, and any other relevant information and documentation which it could reasonably have obtained.

(3)   The possessor shall not be in a more favourable position than the person from whom it acquired the object by inheritance or otherwise gratuitously.

CHAPTER III — RETURN OF ILLEGALLY EXPORTED CULTURAL OBJECTS

Article 5

(1)   A Contracting State may request the court or other competent authority of another Contracting State acting under Article 9 to order the return of a cultural object which has

(a)   been removed from the territory of the requesting State contrary to its law regulating the export of cultural objects because of their cultural significance;

(b)   been temporarily exported from the territory of the requesting State under a permit, for purposes such as exhibition, research or restoration, and not returned in accordance with the terms of that permit [, or

(c)   been taken from a site contrary to the laws of the requesting State applicable to the excavation of cultural objects and removed from that State] .

(2)   The court or other competent authority of the State addressed shall order the return of the object if the requesting State establishes that the removal of the object from its territory significantly impairs one or more of the following interests

(a)   the physical preservation of the object or of its context,

(b)   the integrity of a complex object,

(c)   the preservation of information of, for example, a scientific or historical character,

(d)   the use of the object by a living culture,

or establishes that the object is of outstanding cultural importance for the requesting State.

(3)   Any request made under paragraph 1 shall contain or be accompanied by such information of a factual or legal nature as may assist the court or other competent authority of the State addressed in determining whether the requirements of paragraphs 1 and 2 have been met.

(4)   Any request for return shall be brought within a period of [one] [three] year[s] from the time when the requesting State knew or ought reasonably to have known the location of the object and the identity of its possessor, and in any case within a period of [thirty] [fifty] years from the date of the export.

Article 6

(1)   When the requirements of Article 5, paragraph 2 have been satisfied, the court or other competent authority of the State addressed may only refuse to order the return of a cultural object where

(a)   the object has a closer connection with the culture of the State addressed [, or

(b)   the object, prior to its unlawful removal from the territory of the requesting State, was unlawfully removed from the State addressed].

(2)   The provisions of sub-paragraph (a) of the preceding paragraph shall not apply in the case of objects referred to in Article 5, paragraph 1(b).

Article 7

(1)   The provisions of Article 5, paragraph 1 shall not apply where the export of the cultural object is no longer illegal at the time at which the return is requested.

(2)   Neither shall they apply where

(a)   the object was exported during the lifetime of the person who created it [or within a period of [five] years following the death of that person]; or

(b)   the creator is not known, if the object was less than [twenty] years old at the time of export [;

except where the object was made by a member of an indigenous community for use by that community].

Article 8

(1)   The possessor of a cultural object removed from the territory of a Contracting State contrary to its law regulating the export of cultural objects because of their cultural significance shall be entitled, at the time of the return of the object, to payment by the requesting State of fair and reasonable compensation, provided that the possessor neither knew nor ought reasonably to have known at the time of acquisition that the object had been unlawfully removed.

[(2)   Where a Contracting State has instituted a system of export certificates, the absence of an export certificate for an object for which it is required shall put the purchaser on notice that the object has been illegally exported.]

(3)   Instead of requiring compensation, and in agreement with the requesting State, the possessor may, when returning the object to that State, decide

(a)   to retain ownership of the object; or

(b)   to transfer ownership against payment or gratuitously to a person of its choice residing in the requesting State and who provides the necessary guarantees.

(4)   The cost of returning the object in accordance with this article shall be borne by the requesting State, without prejudice to the right of that State to recover costs from any other person.

(5) The possessor shall not be in a more favourable position than the person from whom it acquired the object by inheritance or otherwise gratuitously.

CHAPTER IV — CLAIMS AND ACTIONS

Article 9

(1)   Without prejudice to the rules concerning jurisdiction in force in Contracting States, the claimant may in all cases bring a claim or request under this Convention before the courts or other competent authorities of the Contracting State where the cultural object is located.

(2)   The parties may also agree to submit the dispute to another jurisdiction or to arbitration.

(3)   Resort may be had to the provisional, including protective, measures available under the law of the Contracting State where the object is located even when the claim for restitution or request for return of the object is brought before the courts or other competent authorities of another Contracting State.

CHAPTER V — FINAL PROVISIONS

Article 10

Nothing in this Convention shall prevent a Contracting State from applying any rules more favourable to the restitution or the return of a stolen or illegally exported cultural object than provided for by this Convention.

APPENDIX V

CONSOLIDATED TABLE OF PARTICIPATION IN ILLICIT TRAFFIC INSTRUMENTS

Key:

*	Party
p	Potentially applies (Commonwealth scheme is to be adopted by national legislation. Model legislation is still in course of preparation)
n	Took part in negotiations (either in some/all of 4 meetings of Governmental Experts and/or Diplomatic Conference)
S	Signed
R	Ratified
A	Acceded

	Hague Protocol	UNESCO Convention 1970	Commonwealth Scheme	European Directive	UNIDROIT 1995
Albania	*				n
Algeria		*			n
Angola		*			n
Antigua & Barbuda			p		
Argentina		*			n
Armenia	*	*			
Australia		*	p		n
Austria	*			*	n
Azerbaijan	*				
Bahamas			p		
Bangladesh		*	p		
Barbados			p		
Belarus	*	*			n
Belgium	*			*	n
Belize		*	p		
Bolivia		*			S
Bosnia-Hzg	*	*			
Botswana			p		

106

Brazil	*	*			n
Brunei Darassalam			p		
Bulgaria	*	*			n
Burkina Faso	*	*			S
Cambodia	*	*			S
Cameroon	*	*	p		n
Canada		*	p		n
Central African Rep.		*			
Chile					n
China		*			A
Colombia		*			n
Costa Rica		*			
Côte d'Ivoire		*			S
Croatia	*	*			S
Cuba	*	*			
Cyprus	*	*	p		n
Czech Rep.	*	*			n
Denmark				*	n
Dominica			p		
Dominican Rep.		*			
Ecuador	*	*			n
Egypt	*	*			n
El Salvador		*			
Estonia		*			
Finland	*			*	S
France	*	*		*	S
Gabon	*				n
Gambia			p		
Georgia	*	*			S
Germany	*			*	n
Ghana	*		p		
Greece	*	*		*	n
Grenada		*	p		
Guatemala	*	*			n
Guinea	*	*			S
Guyana			p		

Holy See	*				n
Honduras		*			
Hungary	*	*			S
India	*	*	p		n
Indonesia	*				n
Iran	*	*			n
Iraq	*	*			
Ireland				*	n
Israel	*				n
Italy	*	*		*	S
Jamaica			p		
Japan					n
Jordan	*	*			
Kazakstan	*				
Kenya			p		
Kiribati			p		
Korea, Democ. Rep.		*			
Korea, Rep. Of		*			n
Kuwait	*	*			n
Kyrkhyz Rep.		*			
Latvia					n
Lebanon	*	*			
Lesotho			p		
Libyan Arab Jam.	*	*			n
Liechtenstein	*				
Lithuania					R
Luxembourg	*			*	n
Macedonia	*	*			
Madagascar	*	*			n
Malawi			p		
Malaysia	*		p		n
Maldives			p		
Mali	*	*			n
Malta			p		n
Mauritania		*			
Mauritius		*	p		n

Mexico	*	*			n
Monaco	*				
Mongolia		*			
Morocco	*				n
Mozambique			p		
Myanmar	*				n
Namibia			p		
Nauru			p		
Nepal		*			n
Netherlands	*			*	S
New Zealand			p		n
Nicaruagua	*	*			
Niger	*	*			
Nigeria	*	*	p		n
Norway	*				n
Oman		*			
Pakistan	*	*	p		S
Panama		*			
Papua New Guinea			p		n
Paraguay					R
Peru	*	*			S
Philippines					n
Poland	*	*			n
Portugal		*		*	S
Qatar		*			
Romania	*	*			S
Russian Federation	*	*			S
St. Kitts & Nevis			p		
St. Lucia			p		
St. Vincent & Grens.			p		
San Marino	*				n
Saudi Arabia		*			
Senegal	*	*			S
Seychelles			p		
Sierra Leone			p		
Singapore			p		

Slovak Republic	*	*			
Slovenia	*	*			n
Solomon Islands			p		
South Africa			p		n
Spain	*	*		*	n
Sri Lanka		*	p		
Swaziland			p		
Sweden	*			*	n
Switzerland	*				S
Syrian Arab Rep.	*	*			
Tajikistan	*	*			
Tanzania, United Rep.		*	p		
Thailand	*				n
Tonga			p		
Trinidad & Tobago			p		
Tunisia	*	*			n
Turkey	*	*			n
Tuvalu			p		
Uganda			p		
Ukraine	*	*			n
United Kingdom			p	*	n
United States		*			n
Uruguay		*			
Uzbekistan	*	*			
Vanuatu			p		
Venezuela					n
Western Samoa			p		
Yemen	*				n
Yugoslavia, Fed. R.	*	*			
Zaire	*	*			
Zambia		*	p		S
Zimbabwe			p		

APPENDIX VI

MEANING OF "INDIGENOUS PEOPLES"
(Extract from United Nations Document E/CN.4/Sub.2/1994/2)

Definition of terms

9.   A number of issues of a general nature have been brought up at sessions of the Working Group on Indigenous Populations. These include questions relating to the definition of the beneficiaries, the scope and meaning of terms and words such as "peoples", "self-determination", "self-government and autonomy", "lands and territories" and "ethnocide and cultural genocide", and the references to collective and individual rights.

10.   It may be noted that the United Nations has adopted no official definition of indigenous peoples. The Special Rapporteur of the Sub-Commission, Jose Martinez Cobo, in his *Study of the Problem of Discrimination against Indigenous Populations* writes:

"379. Indigenous communities, peoples and nations are those which, having a historical continuity with pre-invasion and pre-colonial societies that developed on their territories, consider themselves distinct from other sectors of the societies now prevailing in those territories, or parts of them. They form at present non-dominant sectors of society and are determined to preserve, develop and transmit to future generations their ancestral territories, and their ethnic identity, as the basis of their continued existence as peoples, in accordance with their own cultural patterns, social institutions and legal systems.

"389. This historical continuity may consist of the continuation, for an extended period reaching into the present, of one or more of the following factors:

      (a)   Occupation of ancestral lands, or at least of part of them;

      (b)   Common ancestry with the original occupants of these lands;

      (c)   Culture in general, or in specific manifestations (such as religion, living under a tribal system, membership of an indigenous community, dress, means of livelihood, lifestyle, etc.) ;

      (d)   Language (whether used as the only language, as mother tongue, as the habitual means of communication at home or in the family, or as the main, preferred or habitual, general or normal language) ;

      (e)   Residence in certain parts of the country, or in certain regions of the world;

      (f)   other relevant factors." (E/CN.4/Sub.2/1986/7/Add.4).

11.   These considerations of the Special Rapporteur have served, *inter alia*, as a guide to the Working Group on Indigenous Populations. However, in the interests of flexibility and the openness of its proceedings no formal definition has been prepared by the Working Group.

12.   Note may also be taken of the definition contained in article 1 of International Labour Organisation (ILO) Convention No. 169 which specifies the beneficiaries:

> "1. This Convention applies to:
>
> > (a)   Tribal peoples in independent countries whose social, cultural and economic conditions distinguish them from other sections of the national community, and whose status is regulated wholly or in part by their own customs or traditions or by special laws or regulations;
> >
> > (b)   Peoples in independent countries who are regarded as indigenous on account of their descent from the populations which inhabited the country, or a geographical region to which the country belongs, at the time of conquest or colonisation or the establishment of present State boundaries and who, irrespective of their legal status, retain some or all of their own social, economic, cultural or political institutions.
>
> "2.   Self-identification as indigenous or tribal shall be regarded as a fundamental criterion for determining the groups to which the provisions of this Convention apply.
>
> "3.   The use of the term 'peoples' in this Convention shall not be construed as having any implications as regards the rights which may attach to the term under international law."

13.   Furthermore, it may be noted that the Declaration on the Rights of Persons Belonging to National or Ethnic, Religious and Linguistic Minorities contains no definition of the beneficiaries.

APPENDIX VII

Map on indigenous peoples (see comment on 3(8))

WHERE INDIGENOUS PEOPLES LIVE

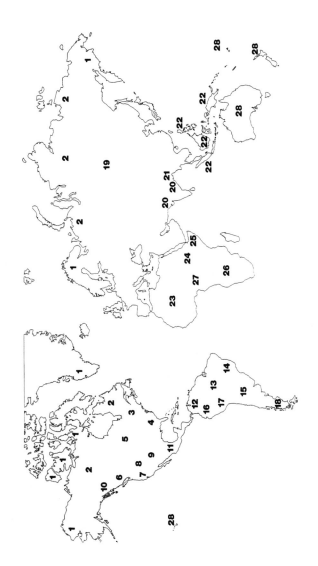

MAP KEY

1. Arctic

Aleut
Chipewyan
Inuit
Saami

2. Sub-Arctic

Cree
Dene
Naskapi
Ojibwa

North America

3. Eastern Woodlands

Algonquin
Haudenosaunee
(Six Nations)
Huron
Micmac
Potawatomi
Shawnee

4. Southeast

Cherokee
Chickasaw
Creek
Seminole

5. Great Plains

Arapaho
Cheyenne
Pawnee
Sioux

6. Northwest Plateau

Nez Perce
Wasco
Yakima

7. California

Cahuillia
Pomo
Serrano

8. Great Basin

Shoshone
Ute

9. Southwest

Apache
Dine (Hopi)
Navajo
Zuni

10. Pacific NW Coast

Bella Coola
Chinook
Haida
Kwakiutl
Salish
Tlingit

11. Central America

Bribri
Cakchiquel
Chol
Chuj
Cora
Guaymi
Huichol
Ixil
Kekchi
Kuna
Lacandon
Lenca
Maya (descendants)
Miskito
Nahua

Pipile
Quiche
Rama
Seri
Sumu
Tarahumara
Yaqui
Yucatec
Zapotec

12. Circum Caribbean

Akawaio
Bari (Motilones)
Choque
Guajiro
Karina
Kogi
Otomac
Paez
Yarawato
Yukpa

South America

13. Amazonia

Aguaruna
Amarakaeri
Aimuesha
Arara
Arawak
Ashaninca
Asurini
Gaviao
Kayapo
Kreen-Akarore
Matsigenka
Mundurucu
Nambikwara
Parakana
Quichua
Sanema
Secoya

Shipibo
Shuar (Jiivaro)
Tukano
Ufaina
Waimiri-Atroari
Waorani (Auca)
Wayana
Xavante
Yagua
Yanomami

14. Mato Grosso

Borboro
Botocudo
Ge (Central)
Guato
Kaduveo
Kaingang
Karaja
Kayapo (Southern)
Tupi

15. Gran Chaco

Ache
Ayoreo
Chamacoco
Chiriguano
Guana
Mataco
Mbaya
Toba-Maskoy

16. W. Andean Lowlands

Cayapas
Colorados

17. Andean Highlands

Aymara
Huancas
Kolla
Mojo
Otavalo
Quechua
Salasaca
Uros

18. Patagonia-Pampas

Aracuanian
Mapuche
Ranquel
Tehuelche

Asia

19. North and Central Asia

Ainu
Hui
Manchu
Miao
Mongolian
Taiwan Aborigenes
Tibetan
Uighur
Yi
Zhuang

20. South Asia

Bhils
Chenchus
Dafflas
Dandami
Gadabas
Garos
Gond
Hos
Irula Kurumbas
Juangs
Kadras
Kameng
Khassis
Khonds
Kolis
Lohit
Mundas
Naga
Oraons
Pathan
Santal
Savaras
Sholegas
Toda Kotas
Vedda

21. Chittagong Hill Tract Peoples

Chakma
Marma
Tripura

22. South East Asia

Chin
Hmong
Kachin
Karen
Kedang
Lisu
Semai
Shan

Africa

23. Sahara, Sahel

Fulani
Tuareg

24. S. Sudan

Dinka
Hamar
Kawahla
Lotuko
Mondari
Nuba
Nuer
Rashaida
Shilluk
Zande

25. The Horn and East Africa

Barabaig
Eriteran
Maasai
Oromo
Somali
Tigrayan

26. Kalahari Desert

San

27. Ituri Forest

Efe
Lese
Mbuti

28. Australia and
   the Pacific

Aboriginals
Arapesh
Asmat
Bangsa
Bontoc
Chainorro
Dani
Dayak
Hanunoo
Hawaiian
Iban
Ifugao
Kalinga
Kanak
Kayan
Kedang
Mae-Enga
Maori
Mundugumur
Penan
Rapa Nui
Tahitian
Torres Strait Islanders
Trsembaga

APPENDIX VIII

SCHEME FOR THE PROTECTION OF CULTURAL HERITAGE WITHIN THE COMMONWEALTH

OBJECTIVES OF THE SCHEME

1.   (1)   The provisions of the Scheme govern the return by one Commonwealth country of an item of cultural heritage found within its jurisdiction following export from another Commonwealth country contrary to its laws.

        (2)   The provisions of the Scheme will apply to the export and import of items which take place after the adoption and implementation of the Scheme. The Scheme adds to and in no way derogates from future and existing means of recovery of items of cultural heritage.

        (3)   The Scheme is intended to be complementary to, and does not in any way exclude, full participation in other international arrangements such as the UNESCO Convention on the Means of Prohibiting and Preventing the Illicit Import, Export and Transfer of Ownership of Cultural Property 1970, the UNIDROIT Convention on Stolen or Illegally Exported Cultural Objects, the European Communities directive on the return of cultural objects unlawfully removed from the territory of a member State and the regulation on the export of cultural goods from member States of the European Community.

DEFINITIONS

2.   For the purposes of the Scheme:

        (a)   "country" means:

                (i)   each sovereign and independent country within the Commonwealth together with dependent territories which that country designates; and

                (ii)   each country within the Commonwealth which, though not sovereign and independent, is not a territory designated for the purposes of the preceding sub-paragraph.

        (b)   "country of export" means the country from which an item covered by the Scheme has been unlawfully exported.

        (c)   "country of location" means the country where an item which has been unlawfully exported is located at the time the provisions of the Scheme are invoked by the country of export for the return of the item.

(d)   "unlawful export" in relation to any country means an item which was exported from that country in contravention of its law: it includes an item which has been taken out of the country of export under a conditional permit and where there has subsequently been a breach of the conditions of the permit, in which event "unlawful export" is deemed to have occurred as of the date of the breach of the condition.

ITEMS COVERED BY THE SCHEME

3.   (1)   The Scheme covers all items of cultural heritage so classified by, and subject to export control by, the country of export.

(2)   Items classified should be of national importance by virtue of one or more of the following criteria:

(a)   the close association of the item with the history or life of the country;

(b)   the aesthetic qualities of the item;

(c)   the value of the item in the study of the arts or the sciences;

(d)   the rarity of the item;

(e)   the spiritual or emotional association of the item with the people of the country or any group or section thereof;

(f)   the archaeological significance of the item.

(3)   Where a country is unable by reason of laws pursuant to other international obligations to extend protection to all such items it shall be open to other countries similarly to restrict the protection they afford to that country under this Scheme.

VALIDATION SYSTEM

4.   (1)   As part of the Scheme, a system of validation may be introduced whereby an intending purchaser of an item of cultural heritage or any other interested person is enabled to request of the central authority of the country of export a validation certificate to the effect that the item is not an unlawful export from that country.

(2)   Such a validation certificate would constitute a complete defence to any claim by the country of export that the item had been unlawfully exported.

(3)   Where an application is made for a validation certificate in respect of any item, the application should be granted or refused within six months of receipt of the

application. If the application is not granted or refused within that period, the country of export should be precluded from claiming that the item has been unlawfully exported from that country.

OPERATION OF THE SCHEME

5. (1) Each country will prohibit the export of items covered by the Scheme except in accordance with the terms of an export permit.

    (2) Each country will take the measures necessary to ensure the return of items covered by the Scheme to the country of export.

6. (1) Each country will designate a central authority for the making and the receiving of requests for the return of items covered by the Scheme.

    (2) Each country will notify the Commonwealth Secretary-General of its central authority.

7. (1) When the country of export learns of the whereabouts of an item covered by the Scheme, it may request the country of location for assistance in the recovery and return of that item.

    (2) Where two countries of export make a request for the return of the same item, the request of the country from which the item was last exported will be proceeded with; but that will not prejudice further requests in respect of the item.

    (3) The request will give sufficient detail to clearly identify the item and where possible its location and shall be accompanied by an official notification from the country of export to the effect that the item is covered by the Scheme and has been unlawfully exported.

    (4) Such notification will be *prima facie* evidence of the matters stated therein.

8. Upon receipt of a request, the country of location will take appropriate steps in accordance with its laws to secure or safeguard the item.

9. (1) The authorities in the country of location may either:

    (a) give notice to the holder of the item that unless court proceedings are commenced within a stipulated period, the item will be returned to the country of export, or

    (b) institute proceedings or advise the country of export to institute proceedings with a view to securing an order for the return of the item to the country of export.

    (2) In any proceedings instituted either by the holder of the item or by the authorities in the country of location or of export the court will determine whether the item is covered by:

       (a)   the Scheme;

       (b)   an export permit; or

       (c)   a validation certificate.

If the item is covered by the Scheme and such a permit or certificate has been issued, or if the item is not covered by the Scheme, the court may order that the item he returned to the holder. If the item is covered by the Scheme and such a permit or certificate has not been issued, the court will order that the item be returned to the country of export.

(3)   Prior to ordering the return of the item the court will determine whether the holder of the item is an innocent purchaser for value having exercised due care and attention in acquiring the item and, if it is proved that the holder is such an innocent purchaser with valid title to the item, the court will order that fair and reasonable compensation be payable by the country of export to the holder as a condition for the return of the item to the country of export. All other questions of title and compensation will be determined by proceedings in the country of export.

(4)   In any proceedings in the country of location, the holder of an item may, unless the contrary be proved, be presumed not to be an innocent purchaser for value if he has neglected or failed to utilise any relevant validation system under the scheme.

10.   The central authority in the country of export to which an item is returned will be required to hold the item for a period of twelve months. During this period it will be open for any person to take proceedings in the country of export to determine any question of title and compensation.

11.   In the event that proceedings to establish title are not commenced within the twelve month period, the central authority will deal with the item in accordance with the law of the country of export.

12.   In any proceedings in a country of location, the court will have due regard to the relevant laws of the country of export.

13.   The person adjudged to have title in the item will not have any right to remove the item from the country of export otherwise than by the process of applying for and obtaining an export permit.

LIMITATION PERIOD

14.   No claim for the return of an item alleged to have been unlawfully exported may be made under the scheme more than five years after the date the country of export had knowledge of the whereabouts of the item in the country of location.

CRIMINAL PROCEEDINGS

15.   Each country:

    (a)   will make it an offence to unlawfully export from its territory an item of its own cultural heritage covered by the Scheme; and

    (b)   may make it an offence to unlawfully import an item of cultural heritage covered by the Scheme unlawfully exported from another country.

COSTS

16.   (1)   The country of location in implementing the Scheme may require the country of export to meet the expenses necessarily incurred in implementing the request of the country of export for the return of any item of cultural heritage.

    (2)   If in the opinion of the country of location the expenses required in order to comply with the request are of an extraordinary nature, that country will consult with the country of export as to the terms and conditions under which compliance with the request may continue, and in the absence of agreement the country of location may refuse to comply further with the request.

STANDARD FORMS

17.   In implementing the Scheme, each country will as far as is practicable use standard forms which will be settled by consultation through the Commonwealth Secretariat.

APPENDIX IX

CONVENTION FOR THE PROTECTION OF CULTURAL PROPERTY IN THE EVENT OF ARMED CONFLICT (THE HAGUE CONVENTION) 1954 AND PROTOCOL

Extract concerning Movable Cultural Property

Article 4. Respect for cultural property

.   .   .

.   .   .

3.   The High Contracting Parties further undertake to prohibit, prevent and, if necessary, put a stop to any form of theft, pillage or misappropriation of, and any acts of vandalism directed against, cultural property. They shall refrain from requisitioning movable cultural property situated in the territory of another High Contracting Party.

.   .   .

.   .   .

Article 18. Application of the Convention

.   .   .

.   .   .

3.   If one of the Powers in conflict is not a Party to the present Convention, the Powers which are Parties thereto shall nevertheless remain bound by it in their mutual relations. They shall furthermore be bound by the Convention, in relation to the said Power, if the latter has declared that it accepts the provisions thereof and so long as it applies to them.

PROTOCOL

The High Contracting Parties are agreed as follows:

1.   Each High Contracting Party undertakes to prevent the exportation, from a territory occupied by it during an armed conflict, of cultural property as defined in Article 1 of the Convention for the Protection of Cultural Property in the Event of Armed Conflict, signed at The Hague on 14 May, 1954.

2.   Each High Contracting Party undertakes to take into its custody cultural property imported into its territory either directly or indirectly from any occupied territory. This shall either be effected automatically upon the importation of the property or, failing this, at the request of the authorities of that territory.

3.   Each High Contracting Party undertakes to return, at the close of hostilities, to the competent authorities of the territory previously occupied, cultural property which is in its territory, if such property has been exported in contravention of the principle laid down in the first paragraph. Such property shall never be retained as war reparations.

4.   The High Contracting Party whose obligation it was to prevent the exportation of cultural property from the territory occupied by it, shall pay an indemnity to the holders in good faith of any cultural property which has to be returned in accordance with the preceding paragraph.

5.   Cultural property coming from the territory of a High Contracting Party and deposited by it in the territory of another High Contracting Party for the purpose of protecting such property against the dangers of an armed conflict, shall be returned by the latter, at the end of hostilities, to the competent authorities of the territory from which it came.

6.   The present Protocol shall bear the date of 14 May, 1954 and, until the date of 31 December, 1954, shall remain open for signature by all States invited to the Conference which met at The Hague from 21 April, 1954 to 14 May, 1954.

7.   (a)   The present Protocol shall be subject to ratification by signatory States in accordance with their respective constitutional procedures.

        (b)   The instruments of ratification shall be deposited with the Director-General of the United Nations Educational, Scientific and Cultural Organization.

8.   From the date of its entry into force, the present Protocol shall be open for accession by all States mentioned in paragraph 6 which have not signed it as well as any other State invited to accede by the Executive Board of the United Nations Educational, Scientific and Cultural Organization. Accession shall be effected by the deposit of an instrument of accession with the Director-General of the United Nations Educational, Scientific and Cultural Organization.

9.   The States referred to in paragraphs 6 and 8 may declare, at the time of signature, ratification or accession, that they will not be bound by the provisions of Section I or by those of Section II of the present Protocol.

10.   (a)   The present Protocol shall enter into force three months after five instruments of ratification have been deposited.

        (b)   Thereafter, it shall enter into force, for each High Contracting Party, three months after the deposit of its instrument of ratification or accession.

        (c)   The situations referred to in Articles 18 and 19 of the Convention for the Protection of Cultural Property in the Event of Armed Conflict, signed at The Hague on 14 May, 1954, shall give immediate effect to ratifications and accessions deposited by the Parties to the conflict either before or after the beginning of hostilities or occupation. In such cases, the Director-General of the United Nations Educational, Scientific and Cultural Organization shall transmit the communications referred to in paragraph 14 by the speediest method.

11. (a) Each State Party to the Protocol on the date of its entry into force shall take all necessary measures to ensure its effective application within a period of six months after such entry into force.

  (b) This period shall be six months from the date of deposit of the instruments of ratification or accession for any State which deposits its instrument of ratification or accession after the date of the entry into force of the Protocol.

12. Any High Contracting Party may, at the time of ratification or accession, or at any time thereafter, declare by notification addressed to the Director-General of the United Nations Educational, Scientific and Cultural Organization, that the present Protocol shall extend to all or any of the territories for whose international relations it is responsible. The said notification shall take effect three months after the date of its receipt.

13. (a) Each High Contracting Party may denounce the present Protocol, on its own behalf, or on behalf of any territory for whose international relations it is responsible.

  (b) The denunciation shall be notified by an instrument in writing, deposited with the Director-General of the United Nations Educational, Scientific and Cultural Organization.

  (c) The denunciation shall take effect one year after receipt of the instrument of denunciation. However, if, on the expiry of this period, the denouncing Party is involved in an armed conflict, the denunciation shall not take effect until the end of hostilities, or until the operations of repatriating cultural property are completed, whichever is the later.

14. The Director-General of the United Nations Educational, Scientific and Cultural Organization shall inform the States referred to in paragraphs 6 and 8, as well as the United Nations, of the deposit of all the instruments of ratification, accession or acceptance provided for in paragraphs 7, 8 and 15 and the notifications and denunciations provided for respectively in paragraphs 12 and 13.

15. (a) The present Protocol may be revised if revision is requested by more than one-third of the High Contracting Parties.

  (b) The Director-General of the United Nations Educational, Scientific and Cultural Organization shall convene a Conference for this purpose.

  (c) Amendments to the present Protocol shall enter into force only after they have been unanimously adopted by the High Contracting Parties represented at the Conference and accepted by each of the High Contracting Parties.

  (d) Acceptance by the High Contracting Parties of amendments to the present Protocol, which have been adopted by the Conference mentioned in subparagraphs (b) and (c), shall be effected by the deposit of a formal instrument with the Director-General of the United Nations Educational, Scientific and Cultural Organization.

(e)   After the entry into force of amendments to the present Protocol, only the text of the said Protocol thus amended shall remain open for ratification or accession.

In accordance with Article 102 of the Charter of the United Nations, the present Protocol shall be registered with the Secretariat of the United Nations at the request of the Director-General of the United Nations Educational, Scientific and Cultural Organization.

IN FAITH WHEREOF the undersigned, duly authorized, have signed the present Protocol.

DONE at The Hague, this fourteenth day of May, 1954, in English, French, Russian and Spanish, the four texts being equally authoritative, in a single copy which shall be deposited in the archives of the United Nations Educational, Scientific and Cultural Organization, and certified true copies of which shall be delivered to all the States referred to in paragraphs 6 and 8 as well as to the United Nations.

APPENDIX X

UNESCO CONVENTION ON THE MEANS OF PROHIBITING AND PREVENTING THE ILLICIT IMPORT, EXPORT AND TRANSFER OF OWNERSHIP OF CULTURAL PROPERTY 1970

The General Conference of the United Nations Educational, Scientific and Cultural Organization, meeting in Paris from 12 October to 14 November 1970, at its sixteenth session,

Recalling the importance of the provisions contained in the Declaration of the Principles of International Cultural Co-operation, adopted by the General Conference at its fourteenth session,

Considering that the interchange of cultural property among nations for scientific cultural and educational purposes increases the knowledge of the civilisation of Man, enriches the cultural life of all peoples and inspires mutual respect and appreciation among nations,

Considering that cultural property constitutes one of the basic elements of civilisation and national culture, and that its true value can be appreciated only in relation to the fullest possible information regarding its origin, history and traditional setting,

Considering that it is incumbent upon every State to protect the cultural property existing within its territory against the dangers of theft, clandestine excavation, and illicit export,

Considering that, to avert these dangers, it is essential for every State to become increasingly alive to the moral obligations to respect its own cultural heritage and that of all nations,

Considering that, as cultural institutions, museums, libraries and archives should ensure that their collections are built up in accordance with universally recognised moral principles,

Considering that the illicit import, export and transfer of ownership of cultural property is an obstacle to that understanding between nations which it is part of Unesco's mission to promote by recommending to interested States, international conventions to this end,

Considering that the protection of cultural heritage can be effective only if organized both nationally and internationally among States working in close co-operation,

Considering that the Unesco General Conference adopted a Recommendation to this effect in 1964,

Having before it further proposals on the means of prohibiting and preventing the illicit import, export and transfer of ownership of cultural property, a question which is on the agenda for the session as item 19,

Having decided, at its fifteenth session, that this question should be made the subject of an international convention,

Adopts this Convention on the fourteenth day of November 1970.

Article 1

For the purposes of this Convention, the term "cultural property" means property which, on religious or secular grounds, is specifically designated by each State as being of importance for archaeology, prehistory, history, literature, art or science and which belongs to the following categories:

(a) Rare collections and specimens of fauna, flora, minerals and anatomy, and objects of palaeontological interest;

(b) property relating to history, including the history of science and technology and military and social history, to the life of national leaders, thinkers, scientists and artists and to events of national importance;

(c) products of archaeological excavations (including regular and clandestine) or of archaeological discoveries;

(d) elements of artistic or historical monuments or archaeological sites which have been dismembered;

(e) antiquities more than one hundred years old, such as inscriptions, coins and engraved seals;

(f) objects of ethnological interest;

(g) property of artistic interest, such as:

   (i) pictures, paintings and drawings produced entirely by hand on any support and in any material (excluding industrial designs and manufactured articles decorated by hand);

   (ii) original works of statuary art and sculpture in any material;

   (iii) original engravings, prints and lithographs;

   (iv) original artistic assemblages and montages in any material;

(h) rare manuscripts and incunabula, old books, documents and publications of special interest (historical, artistic, scientific, literary, etc.) singly or in collections

(i) postage, revenue and similar stamps, singly or in collections;

(j) archives, including sound, photographic and cinematographic archives;

(k) articles of furniture more than one hundred years old and old musical instruments.

Article 2

1.   The States Parties to this Convention recognize that the illicit import, export and transfer of ownership of cultural property is one of the main causes of the impoverishment of the cultural heritage of the countries of origin of such property and that international co-operation constitutes one of the most efficient means of protecting each country's cultural property against all the dangers resulting therefrom.

2.   To this end, the States Parties undertake to oppose such practices with the means at their disposal, and particularly by removing their causes, putting a stop to current practices, and by helping to make the necessary reparations.

Article 3

The import, export or transfer of ownership of cultural property effected contrary to the provisions adopted under this Convention by the States Parties thereto, shall be illicit.

Article 4

The States Parties to this Convention recognize that for the purpose of the Convention property which belongs to the following categories forms part of the cultural heritage of each State:

(a)   Cultural property created by the individual or collective genius of nationals of the State concerned, and cultural property of importance to the State concerned created within the territory of that State by foreign nationals or stateless persons resident within such territory;

(b)   cultural property found within the national territory;

(c)   cultural property acquired by archaeological, ethnological or natural science missions, with the consent of the competent authorities of the country of origin of such property;

(d)   cultural property which has been the subject of a freely agreed exchange;

(e)   cultural property received as a gift or purchased legally with the consent of the competent authorities of the country of origin of such property.

Article 5

To ensure the protection of their cultural property against illicit import, export and transfer of ownership, the States Parties to this Convention undertake, as appropriate for each country, to set up within their territories one or more national services, where such services do not already exist, for the protection of the cultural heritage, with a qualified staff sufficient in number for the effective carrying out of the following functions:

(a)   contributing to the formation of draft laws and regulations designed to secure the protection of the cultural heritage and particularly prevention of the illicit import, export and transfer of ownership of important cultural property;

(b)   establishing and keeping up to date, on the basis of a national inventory of protected property, a list of important public and private cultural property whose export would constitute an appreciable impoverishment of the national cultural heritage;

(c)   promoting the development or the establishment of scientific and technical institutions (museums, libraries, archives, laboratories, workshops . . .) required to ensure the preservation and presentation of cultural property;

(d)   organizing the supervision of archaeological excavations, ensuring the preservation 'in situ' of certain cultural property, and protecting certain areas reserved for future archaeological research;

(e)   establishing, for the benefit of those concerned (curators, collectors, antique dealers, etc.) rules in conformity with the ethical principles set forth in this Convention; and taking steps to ensure the observance of those rules;

(f)   taking educational measures to stimulate and develop respect for the cultural heritage of all States, and spreading knowledge of the provisions of this Convention;

(g)   seeing that appropriate publicity is given to the disappearance of any items of cultural property.

Article 6

The States Parties to this Convention undertake:

(a)   To introduce an appropriate certificate in which the exporting State would specify that the export of the cultural property in question is authorized. The certificate should accompany all items of cultural property exported in accordance with the regulations;

(b)   to prohibit the exportation of cultural property from their territory unless accompanied by the above-mentioned export certificate;

(c)   to publicise this prohibition by appropriate means, particularly among persons likely to export or import cultural property.

Article 7

The States Parties to this Convention undertake:

(a)   To take the necessary measures, consistent with national legislation, to prevent museums and similar institutions within their territories from acquiring cultural property originating in another State Party which has been illegally exported after entry into force of this Convention, in the States concerned. Whenever possible, to inform a State of origin Party to this Convention of an offer of such cultural property illegally removed from that State after the entry into force of this Convention in both States;

(b)   (i)   to prohibit the import of cultural property stolen from a museum or a religious or secular public monument or similar institution in another State Party to this Convention after the entry into force of this Convention for the States concerned, provided that such property is documented as appertaining to the inventory of that institution;

(ii)   at the request of the State Party of origin, to take appropriate steps to recover and return any such cultural property imported after the entry into force of this Convention in both States concerned, provided, however, that the requesting State shall pay just compensation to an innocent purchaser or to a person who has valid title to that property. Requests for recovery and return shall be made through diplomatic offices. The requesting Party shall furnish, at its expense, the documentation and other evidence necessary to establish its claim for recovery and return. The Parties shall impose no customs duties or other charges upon cultural property returned pursuant to this Article. All expenses incident to the return and delivery of the cultural property shall be borne by the requesting Party.

Article 8

The States Parties to this Convention undertake to impose penalties or administrative sanctions on any person responsible for infringing the prohibitions referred to under Articles 6(b) and 7(b) above.

Article 9

Any State Party to this Convention whose cultural patrimony is in jeopardy from pillage of archaeological or ethnological materials may call upon other States Parties who are affected. The States Parties to this Convention undertake, in these circumstances, to participate in a concerted international effort to determine and to carry out the necessary concrete measures, including the control of exports and imports and international commerce in the specific materials concerned. Pending agreement each State concerned shall take provisional measures to the extent feasible to prevent irremediable injury to the cultural heritage of the requesting State.

Article 10

The States Parties to this Convention undertake:

(a)   To restrict by education, information and vigilance, movement of cultural property illegally removed from any State Party to this Convention and, as appropriate for each country, oblige antique dealers, subject to penal or administrative sanctions, to maintain a register recording the origin of each item of cultural property, names and addresses of the supplier, description and price of each item sold and to inform the purchaser of the cultural property of the export prohibition to which such property may be subject;

(b)   to endeavour by educational means to create and develop in the public mind a realisation of the value of cultural property and the threat to the cultural heritage created by theft, clandestine excavations and illicit exports.

Article 11

The export and transfer of ownership of cultural property under compulsion arising directly or indirectly from the occupation of a country by a foreign power shall be regarded as illicit.

Article 12

The States Parties to this Convention shall respect the cultural heritage within the territories for the international relations of which they are responsible, and shall take all appropriate measures to prohibit and prevent the illicit import, export and transfer of ownership of cultural property in such territories.

Article 13

The States Parties to this Convention also undertake, consistent with the laws of each State:

(a)   To prevent by all appropriate means transfers of ownership of cultural property likely to promote the illicit import or export of such property;

(b)   to ensure that their competent services co-operate in facilitating the earliest possible restitution of illicitly exported cultural property to its rightful owner;

(c)   to admit actions for recovery of lost or stolen items of cultural property brought by or on behalf of the rightful owners;

(d)   to recognize the indefeasible right of each State Party to this Convention to classify and declare certain cultural property as inalienable which should therefore *ipso facto* not be exported, and to facilitate recovery of such property by the State concerned in cases where it has been exported.

Article 14

In order to prevent illicit export and to meet the obligations arising from the implementation of this Convention, each State Party to the Convention should, as far as it is able, provide the national services responsible for the protection of its cultural heritage with an adequate budget and, if necessary, should set up a fund for this purpose.

Article 15

Nothing in this Convention shall prevent States Parties thereto from concluding special agreements among themselves or from continuing to implement agreements already concluded regarding the restitution of cultural property removed, whatever the reason, from its territory of origin, before the entry into force of this Convention for the States concerned.

Article 16

The States Parties to this Convention shall in their periodic reports submitted to the General Conference of the United Nations Educational, Scientific and Cultural Organization on dates and in a manner to be determined by it, give information on the legislative and administrative provisions which they have adopted and other action which they have taken for the application of this Convention, together with details of the experience acquired in this field.

Article 17

1.   The States Parties to this Convention may call on the technical assistance of the United Nations Educational, Scientific and Cultural Organization, particularly as regards:

(a)   Information and education;

(b)   consultation and expert advice;

(c)   co-ordination and good offices.

2.   The United Nations Educational, Scientific and Cultural Organization may, on its own initiative conduct research and publish studies on matters relevant to the illicit movement of cultural property.

3.   To this end, the United Nations Educational, Scientific and Cultural Organization may also call on the co-operation of any competent non-governmental organization.

4.   The United Nations Educational, Scientific and Cultural Organization may, on its own initiative, make proposals to States Parties to this Convention for its implementation.

5.   At the request of at least two States Parties to this Convention which are engaged in a dispute over its implementation, Unesco may extend its good offices to reach a settlement between them.

Article 18

This Convention is drawn up in English, French, Russian and Spanish, the four texts being equally authoritative.

Article 19

1.   This Convention shall be subject to ratification or acceptance by States members of the United Nations Educational, Scientific and Cultural Organization in accordance with their respective constitutional procedures.

2.   The instruments of ratification or acceptance shall be deposited with the Director-General of the United Nations Educational, Scientific and Cultural Organization.

Article 20

1.   This Convention shall be open to accession by all States not members of the United Nations Educational, Scientific and Cultural Organization which are invited to accede to it by the Executive Board of the Organization.

2.   Accession shall be effected by the deposit of an instrument of accession with the Director-General of the United Nations Educational, Scientific and Cultural Organization.

Article 21

This Convention shall enter into force three months after the date of the deposit of the third instrument of ratification, acceptance or accession, but only with respect to those States which have deposited their respective instruments on or before that date. It shall enter into force with respect to any other State three months after the deposit of its instrument of ratification, acceptance or accession.

Article 22

The States Parties to this Convention recognize that the Convention is applicable not only to their metropolitan territories but also to all territories for the international relations of which they are responsible; they undertake to consult, if necessary, the governments or other competent authorities of these territories on or before ratification, acceptance or accession with a view to securing the application of the Convention to those territories, and to notify the Director-General of the United Nations Educational, Scientific and Cultural Organization of the territories to which it is applied, the notification to take effect three months after the date of its receipt.

Article 23

1.   Each State Party to this Convention may denounce the Convention on its own behalf or on behalf of any territory for whose international relations it is responsible.

2.   The denunciation shall be notified by an instrument in writing, deposited with the Director-General of the United Nations Educational, Scientific and Cultural Organization.

3.   The denunciation shall take effect twelve months after the receipt of the instrument of denunciation.

Article 24

The Director-General of the United Nations Educational, Scientific and Cultural Organization shall inform the States members of the Organization, the States not members of the Organization which are referred to in Article 20, as well as the United Nations, of the deposit of all the instruments of ratification, acceptance and accession provided for in Articles 19 and 20, and of the notifications and denunciations provided for in Articles 22 and 23 respectively.

Article 25

1. This Convention may be revised by the General Conference of the United Nations Educational, Scientific and Cultural Organization. Any such revision shall, however, bind only the States which shall become Parties to the revising convention.

2. If the General Conference should adopt a new convention revising this Convention in whole or in part, then, unless the new convention otherwise provides, this Convention shall cease to be open to ratification, acceptance or accession, as from the date on which the new revising convention enters into force.

Article 26

In conformity with Article 102 of the Charter of the United Nations, this Convention shall be registered with the Secretariat of the United Nations at the request of the Director-General of the United Nations Educational, Scientific and Cultural Organization.

Done in Paris this seventeenth day of November 1970, in two authentic copies bearing the signature of the President of the sixteenth session of the General Conference and of the Director-General of the United Nations Educational, Scientific and Cultural Organization, which shall be deposited in the archives of the United Nations Educational, Scientific and Cultural Organization, and certified true copies of which shall be delivered to all the States referred to in Articles 19 and 20 as well as to the United Nations.

The foregoing is the authentic text of the Convention duly adopted by the General Conference of the United Nations Educational, Scientific and Cultural Organization during its sixteenth session, which was held in Paris and declared closed the fourteenth day of November 1970.

IN FAITH WHEREOF we have appended our signatures this seventeenth day of November 1970.

The President of the General Conference   The Director-General

Entered into force 24 April 1972.

APPENDIX XI

EUROPEAN DIRECTIVE OF 15 MARCH 1993 ON THE RETURN OF CULTURAL OBJECTS UNLAWFULLY REMOVED FROM THE TERRITORY OF A MEMBER STATE

COUNCIL DIRECTIVE 93/7/EEC

of 15 March 1993

On the return of cultural objects unlawfully removed
from the territory of a Member State.

THE COUNCIL OF THE EUROPEAN COMMUNITIES,

Having regard to the Treaty establishing the European Economic Community, and in particular Article 100a thereof,

Having regard to the proposal from the Commission[1],

In cooperation with the European Parliament[2],

Having regard to the opinion of the Economic and Social Committee[3],

Whereas Article 8a of the Treaty provides for the establishment, not later than 1 January 1993, of the internal market, which is to comprise an area without internal frontiers in which the free movement of goods, persons, services and capital is ensured in accordance with the provisions of the Treaty;

Whereas, under the terms and within the limits of Article 36 of the Treaty, Member States will, after 1992, retain the right to define their national treasures and to take the necessary measures to protect them in this area without internal frontiers;

Whereas arrangements should therefore be introduced enabling Member States to secure the return to their territory of cultural objects which are classified as national treasures within the meaning of the said Article 36 and have been removed from their territory in breach of the abovementioned national measures or of Council Regulation (EEC) No 3911/92 of 9 December 1992 on the export of cultural goods[4]; whereas the implementation of these arrangements should be as simple and efficient as possible; whereas, to facilitate cooperation with regard to return, the scope of the arrangements should be confined to items belonging to common categories of cultural object; whereas the Annex to this Directive is consequently not intended to define objects which rank as 'national treasures' within the meaning of the said Article 36, but merely categories of object which may be classified as such and may accordingly be covered by the return procedure introduced by this Directive;

Whereas cultural objects classified as national treasures and forming an integral part of public collections or inventories of ecclesiastical institutions but which do not fall within these common categories should also be covered by this Directive;

Whereas administrative cooperation should be established between Member States as regards their national treasures, in close liaison with their cooperation in the field of stolen works of art and involving in particular the recording, with INTERPOL and other qualified bodies issuing similar lists, of lost, stolen or illegally removed cultural objects forming part of their national treasures and their public collections;

Whereas the procedure introduced by this Directive is a first step in establishing cooperation between Member States in this field in the context of the internal market; whereas the aim is mutual recognition of the relevant national laws; whereas provision should therefore be made, in particular, for the Commission to be assisted by an advisory committee;

Whereas Regulation (EEC) No 3911/92 introduces, together with this Directive, a Community system to protect Member States' cultural goods ; whereas the date by which Member States have to comply with this Directive has to be as close as possible to the date of entry into force of that Regulation; whereas, having regard to the nature of their legal systems and the scope of the changes to their legislation necessary to implement this Directive, some Member States will need a longer period,

HAS ADOPTED THIS DIRECTIVE :

Article 1

For the purposes of this Directive:

1. 'Cultural object' shall mean an object which :

- is classified, before or after its unlawful removal from the territory of a Member State, among the 'national treasures possessing artistic, historic or archaeological value' under national legislation or administrative procedures within the meaning of Article 36 of the Treaty,

and

- belongs to one of the categories listed in the Annex or does not belong to one of these categories but forms an integral part of :

- public collections listed in the inventories of museums, archives or libraries' conservation collection.

For the purposes of this Directive, 'public collections' shall mean collections which are the property of a Member State, local or regional authority within a Member State or an institution situated in the territory of a Member State and defined as public in accordance with the legislation of that Member State, such institution being the property of, or significantly financed by, that Member State or a local or regional authority;

- the inventories of ecclesiastical institutions.

2. 'Unlawfully removed from the territory of a Member State' shall mean:

- removed from the territory of a Member State in breach of its rules on the protection of national treasures or in breach of Regulation (EEC) No 3911/92, or

- not returned at the end of a period of lawful temporary removal or any breach of another condition governing such temporary removal.

3. 'Requesting Member State' shall mean the Member State from whose territory the cultural object has been unlawfully removed.

4. 'Requested Member State' shall mean the Member State in whose territory a cultural object unlawfully removed from the territory of another Member State is located.

5. 'Return' shall mean the physical return of the cultural object to the territory of the requesting Member State.

6. 'Possessor' shall mean the person physically holding the cultural object on his own account.

7. 'Holder' shall mean the person physically holding the cultural object for third parties.

Article 2

Cultural objects which have been unlawfully removed from the territory of a Member State shall be returned in accordance with the procedure and in the circumstances provided for in this Directive.

Article 3

Each Member State shall appoint one or more central authorities to carry out the tasks provided for in this Directive.

Member States shall inform the Commission of all the central authorities they appoint pursuant to this Article.

The Commission shall publish a list of these central authorities and any changes concerning them in the 'C' series of the *Official Journal of the European Communities*.

Article 4

Member States' central authorities shall cooperate and promote consultation between the Member States' competent national authorities. The latter shall in particular:

1. upon application by the requesting Member State, seek a specified cultural object which has been unlawfully removed from its territory, identifying the possessor and/or holder. The application must include all information needed to facilitate this search, with particular

reference to the actual or presumed location of the object;

2. notify the Member States concerned, where a cultural object is found in their own territory and there are reasonable grounds for believing that it has been unlawfully removed from the territory of another Member State;

3. enable the competent authorities of the requesting Member State to check that the object in question is a cultural object provided that the check is made within 2 months of the notification provided for in paragraph 2. If it is not made within the stipulated period, paragraphs 4 and 5 shall cease to apply;

4. take any necessary measures, in cooperation with the Member State concerned, for the physical preservation of the cultural object;

5. prevent by the necessary interim measures, any action to evade the return procedure;

6. act as intermediary between the possessor and/or holder and the requesting Member State with regard to return. To this end, the competent authorities of the requested Member States may, without prejudice to Article 5, first facilitate the implementation of an arbitration procedure, in accordance with the national legislation of the requested State and provided that the requesting State and the possessor or holder give their formal approval.

Article 5

The requesting Member State may initiate, before the competent court in the requested Member State, proceedings against the possessor or, failing him, the holder, with the aim of securing the return of a cultural object which has been unlawfully removed from its territory.

Proceedings may be brought only where the document initiating them is accompanied by :

- a document describing the object covered by the request and stating that it is a cultural object,

- a declaration by the competent authorities of the requesting Member State that the cultural object has been unlawfully removed from its territory.

Article 6

The central authority of the requesting Member State shall forthwith inform the central authority of the requested Member State that proceedings have been initiated with the aim of securing the return of the object in question.

The central authority of the requested Member State shall forthwith inform the central authorities of the other Member States.

Article 7

1. Member States shall lay down in their legislation that the return proceedings provided for in this Directive may not be brought more than one year after the requesting Member State became aware of the location of the cultural object and of the identity of its possessor or holder.
Such proceedings may, at all events, not be brought more than 30 years after the object was unlawfully removed from the territory of the requesting Member State. However, in the case of objects forming part of public collections, referred in Article 1 (1), and ecclesiastical goods in the Member States where they are subject to special protection arrangements under national law, return proceedings shall be subject to a time-limit of 75 years , except in Member States where proceedings are not subject to a time-limit or in the case of bilateral agreements between Member States laying down a period exceeding 75 Years.

2. Return proceedings may not be brought if removal from the national territory of the requesting Member State is no longer unlawful at the time when they are to be initiated.

Article 8

Save as otherwise provided in Articles 7 and 13, the competent court shall order the return of the cultural object in question where it is found to be a cultural object within the meaning of Article 1(1) and to have been removed unlawfully from national territory.

Article 9

Where return of the object is ordered, the competent court in the requested States shall award the possessor such compensation as it deems fair according to the circumstances of the case, provided that it is satisfied that the possessor exercised due care and attention in acquiring the object.

The burden of proof shall be governed by the legislation of the requested Member State.

In the case of a donation or succession, the possessor shall not be in a more favourable position than the person from whom he acquired the object by that means.

The requesting Member State shall pay such compensation upon return of the object.

Article 10

Expenses incurred in implementing a decision ordering the return of a cultural object shall be borne by the requesting Member State. The same applies to the costs of the measures referred to Article 4(4).

Article 11

Payment of the fair compensation and of the expenses referred to in Articles 9 and 10 respectively shall be without prejudice to the requesting Member State's right to take action with a view to recovering those amounts from the persons responsible for the unlawful removal of the cultural object from its territory.

Article 12

Ownership of the cultural object after return shall be governed by that law of the requesting Member State.

Article 13

This Directive shall apply only to cultural objects unlawfully removed from the territory of a Member State on or after 1 January 1993.

Article 14

1. Each Member State may extend its obligation to return cultural objects to cover categories of objects other than those listed in the Annex.

2. Each Member State may apply the arrangements provided for by this Directive to requests for the return of cultural objects unlawfully removed from the territory of other Member States prior to 1 January 1993.

Article 15

This Directive shall be without prejudice to any civil or criminal proceedings that may be brought, under the national laws of the Member States, by the requesting Member State and/or the owner of a cultural object that has been stolen.

Article 16

1. Member States shall send the Commission every three years, and for the first time in February 1996, a report on the application of this Directive.

2. The Commission shall send the European Parliament, the Council and the Economic and Social Committee, every three years, a report reviewing the application of this Directive.

3. The Council shall review the effectiveness of this Directive after a period of application of three years and, acting on a proposal from the Commission, make any necessary adaptations.

4. In any event, the Council acting on a proposal from the Commission, shall examine every three years and, where appropriate, update the amounts indicated in the Annex, on the basis of economic and monetary indicators in the Community.

Article 17

The Commission shall be assisted by the Committee set up by Article 8 of Regulation (EEC) No 3911/92.

The Committee shall examine any questions arising from the application of the Annex to this Directive which may be tabled by the chairman either on his own initiative or at the request of the representative of a Member State.

Article 18

Member States shall bring into force the laws, regulations and administrative provisions necessary to comply with this Directive within nine months of its adoption, except as far as the Kingdom of Belgium, the Federal Republic of Germany and the Kingdom of the Netherlands are concerned, which must conform to this Directive at the latest twelve months from the date of its adoption. They shall forthwith inform the Commission thereof.

When Member States adopt these measures, they shall contain a reference to this Directive or shall be accompanied by such reference on the occasion of their official publication. The methods of making such a reference shall be laid down by the Member States.

Article 19

This Directive is addressed to the Member States.

Done at Brussels, 15 March 1993

1   OJ No C 53, 28. 2. 1992, p. 11, and OJ No C 172, 8. 7. 1992, p. 7.
2   OJ No C 176, 13. 7. 1992, p. 129 and OJ No C 72, 15. 3. 1993.
3   OJ No C 223, 31. 8. 1992, p. 10.
4   OJ No L 395, 31. 12. 1992, p. 1.

Annex

Categories referred to in the second indent of Article 1 (1) to which objects classified as 'national treasures' within the meaning of Article 36 of the Treaty must belong in order to qualify for return under this Directive.

A. 1. Archaeological objects more than 100 years old which are the products of:
-land or underwater excavations and finds,
-archaeological sites,
-archaeological collections.

2. Elements forming an integral part of artistic, historical or religious monuments which have been dismembered, more than 100 years old.

3. Pictures and paintings executed entirely by hand, on any medium and in any material[1].

4. Mosaics; other than those in category 1 or category 2 and drawings executed entirely by hand, on any medium and in any material[1].

5. Original engravings, prints, serigraphs and lithographs with their respective plates and

original posters[1].

6. Original sculptures or statuary and copies produced by the same process as the original (1) other than those in category 1.

7. Photographs, films and negatives thereof[1].

8. Incunabula and manuscripts, including maps and musical scores, singly or in collections[1].

9. Books more than 100 years old, singly or in collections.

10. Printed maps more than 200 years old.

11. Archives and any elements thereof, of any kind, on any medium, comprising elements more than 50 years old.

12. (a) Collections[2] and specimens from zoological, botanical, mineralogical or anatomical collections;

      (b) Collections[2] of historical, palaeontological, ethnographic or numismatic interest.

13. Means of transport more than 75 years old.

14. Any other antique item not included in categories A1 to A13, more than 50 years old.

The cultural objects in categories A1 to A14 are covered by this Directive only if their value corresponds to, or exceeds, the financial thresholds under B.

B Financial thresholds applicable to certain categories under A (in Ecus)

VALUE: **0 (Zero)**

- 1 (Archaeological objects)
- 2 (Dismembered monuments)
- 8 (Incunabula and manuscripts)
- 11 (Archives)

15,000

- 4 (Mosaics and drawings)
- 5 (Engravings)
- 7 (Photographs)
-10 (Printed maps)

50,000

- 6 (Statuary)
- 9 (Books)
- 12 (Collections)
- 13 (Means of transport)

- 14 (Any other item)

150,000

- 3 (Pictures)

The assessment of whether or not the conditions relating to financial value are fulfilled must be made when return is requested. The financial value is that of the object in the requested Member State.

The date for the conversion of the values expressed in ecus in the Annex into national currencies shall be 1 January 1993.

---

1. Which are more than fifty years old and do not belong to their originators.
2. As defined by the Court of justice in its Judgment in Case 252/84, as follows:
   'Collectors' pieces within the meaning of Heading No 99.05 of the Common Customs Tariff are articles which possess the requisite characteristics for inclusion in a collection, that is to say, articles which are relatively rare, are not normally used for their original purpose, are the subject of special transactions outside the normal trade in similar utility articles and are of high value.

APPENDIX XII

In *De Préval v. Adrian Alan Ltd.*, unreported decision of Arden J. Q.B.D. 24 January 1997 [United Kingdom], the French plaintiff sued for the return of two French gilt-bronze champlevé enamel candelabra which had been stolen in France in 1986. They were part of a triptych modelled specially for her great great-grandfather by Antoine-Louis Barye in Paris in about 1846.

The defendant company, an antique dealer, claimed to have bought them in New York in 1984, but could bring no documentary evidence to this effect. The Limitation Act 1980 in force in England prescribes a limitation of six years for claims for movables, dating from a conversion (i.e. acquisition) not related to the theft. For the defendant to take advantage of this limitation it had to prove that the acquisition had been in good faith.

Expert evidence was given that after Barye's death many of his moulds were sold to Barbedienne who specialized in enamel: it was therefore possible that the stolen candelabra had been made by him. However, the only significant enamelled bronze pieces by Barye known were those made for Emile Martin and the pieces in question featured the initials "E" and "M" and the insignia of the Légion d'Honneur. The quality of the enamelling also suggested to the expert that the candelabra in question were made by Barye and not by Barbedienne. Other experts gave evidence that enamelled objects identical to these had never been seen on the market. The judge held that it was most unlikely that some previously unknown candelabra, made with Emile Martin's initials and insignia, would have come to light around the time of the theft of the stolen candelabra.

The principal shareholder and director of the defendant company said that he was not aware of the link to Barye when he bought the candelabra. The judge held that a dealer of his experience would know about Barye and realise that these candelabra were unusual and rather special. His evidence had shown that he had looked for a signature. The judge held that, as the defendant had not shown that he had no reason to doubt that the dealer would have title to the candelabra to sell to him, the limitation period could not be used against the plaintiff who was able to recover the stolen property.

The judgment therefore illustrates that in such a case the dealer should have made an effort to verify the title. If a private collector or amateur had made the purchase, it is reasonable to expect that, considering the value of the candelabra (the purchaser said that he had paid between $5,000 and $6,000 in 1984 in New York, and they were valued in London by a Sotheby's expert as worth £60,000 in 1994), he or she would, in common prudence, seek expert opinion or make the purchase through a dealer who would make the necessary inquiries. Failure to do so would mean that compensation under the UNIDROIT Convention would be unlikely to be awarded.

The case is discussed in detail in Redmond-Cooper, R. "Good Faith Acquisition of Stolen Art" 2 *Art Antiquity and Law* (1997) 55-61.

APPENDIX XIII

In *Autocephalous Greek-Orthodox Church v. Goldberg* the judge at first instance made findings of fact on the good faith of the defendant which would have been relevant had Swiss law been held applicable (in fact, he held that Indiana law applied and this was upheld on appeal). In finding against good faith, the judge took the following factors into account:

* the defendant knew that the mosaics came from an area under military occupation;
* the mosaics were unique, of great cultural and artistic as well as commercial value, and objects of religious significance which do not ordinarily enter into commerce;
* there was vast disparity between the appraised value of the mosaics and the price paid (as well as the price for which the defendant subsequently offered them);
* the defendant knew very little about the seller, but knew that he was a Moslem Turk selling Christian objects from Northern Cyprus; that he claimed to be an archaeologist but was selling antiquities; she met him only once and he had produced no documents of title;
* she knew very little about the three middlemen, but did know that one was a convicted felon and that another had used several aliases;
* the transaction was carried out in great haste;
* claims of the defendant to have made inquiries of UNESCO and IFAR were not substantiated by the evidence;
* no inquiry was made of Cyprus, of any independent expert in Byzantine mosaics, of the authorities in control in Northern Cyprus nor of INTERPOL.